New Macroeconomics

New Macroeconomics

Apek Mulay

BUSINESS EXPERT PRESS

New Macroeconomics
Copyright © Business Expert Press, LLC, 2018.

First published in 2018 by
Business Expert Press, LLC
222 East 46th Street, New York, NY 10017
www.businessexpertpress.com

ISBN-13: 978-1-94744-112-5 (paperback)
ISBN-13: 978-1-94744-113-2 (e-book)

Business Expert Press Economics Collection

Collection ISSN: 2163-761X (print)
Collection ISSN: 2163-7628 (electronic)

Cover and interior design by S4Carlisle Publishing Services Private Ltd., Chennai, India

First edition: 2018

10 9 8 7 6 5 4 3 2 1

Printed in the United States of America.

Dedication

This book is dedicated to my parents
—Dr. Pradeep S. Mulay and Dr. Prajkta P. Mulay

Abstract

According to the National Bureau of Economic Research (NBER), a deep recession started in the United States in December 2007 and ended in June 2009. However, most people recognize that even though the recession was said to be over, its aftereffects lingered well into the next decade, and even in 2017, some ten years later, governments in America and around the world were struggling with problems of low growth, wage stagnation, and high poverty.

Most economists were caught off guard, and they began to look for new ideas that may be appropriately called NEW MACROECONOMICS.

In the spirit of scientific inquiry, it is important to compare accepted theory with reality. Keynesianism remains the dominant paradigm in macroeconomics, and the 2008 meltdown revived Keynesian prescriptions. But the subsequent anemic and fraught recovery also intensified criticism of Keynesianism. This book examines consensus economics in the context of recent developments.

I confess that this book could be interpreted as a highly personal perspective. It draws upon ideas from a few well-known experts such as Professors Joseph Stiglitz, Paul Krugman, and Ravi Batra through the lens of my own experience in the technology sector. The book shows that a new theory, known as the wage-productivity model, explains almost every macroeconomic experience of the global economy since 1980. This is an incredible claim, but those who have examined it agree with my assessment. The forecasting record of this theory is also stunning. It predicted the Great Recession a year before it started, arguing that a steep downturn would start in 2007 and then linger in one form or another until 2019. You have to read this theory to believe it.

Keywords

The environment, free markets, the Great Recession, negative interest rates, stock market bubble and crash, wealth concentration

Contents

Foreword

It is with great pleasure that I write this foreword on *New Macroeconomics* by Mr. Apek Mulay. Rarely have I seen a book that meets the needs of the times. The major economic crisis that shook the United States and the globe in 2007 also shook the field of economics. By then, most economists had come to accept the idea that business cycles were a thing of the past. Macroeconomists, essentially bored with their own subject, had busied themselves with microeconomic foundations. There had been no serious slump since the early 1980s. There were indeed several stock market bubbles and crashes rivaling the crash of 1929 that spawned the Great Depression. However, nothing like the slump of the 1930s had occurred since World War II.

Even the crash of October 19, 1987, when the Dow Jones Index fell by 22.5 percent, in just one day, had come and gone without creating a recession. The crashes of 2000 to 2001 had also passed with barely a ripple in the global economy. Not surprisingly, economists came to believe in the basic stability of modern-day capitalism. They ignored the mushrooming imbalances such as growing consumer and government debt, high trade deficits and surpluses, rocketing income, and wealth disparities. They also ignored that industry after industry had become an oligopoly, stifling competition that fuels efficiency and economic growth.

The Great Recession of 2007 occurred in the background of vast complacency among economists, especially those in charge of economic policy. The profession has gone through much soul-searching ever since, but as Mr. Mulay notes in this book, the confusion among economists has only grown with no consensus among them about proper macroeconomic theory and policy.

Mr. Mulay is not a degreed economist, and it is a virtue; he has no prior agenda, but has plenty of common sense. He is an engineer by profession, and a really good one. He already has one patent registered in his name during his employment with Texas Instruments, Inc. Apek was introduced to me in 2010, and I was intrigued that he, an engineer, was very interested in understanding what had gone wrong with the global economy after 2007. I informally accepted him as a student, and soon we became good friends. I found him to be very intelligent and hardworking. We talked a few times, and soon he began to comprehend how a macro economy works, so much so that he ended up writing and publishing several articles on the failure of the U.S. economy, using his background as a failure-analysis engineer.

Apek's success as a writer continued. In 2014, he authored a book titled *Mass Capitalism: A Blueprint for Economic Revival.* Once again, he combined his engineering background with his newly discovered interest in macroeconomics in the context of a global economy. He wrote two sequels to this book, and *New Macroeconomics* is his latest, and in my view the best work he has authored so far.

Many new ideas have emerged since 2007 and Mr. Mulay weaves them together in a coherent theme. He argues that conventional economic theories are broken because they ignore the vast amount of debt they generate. Some theories emphasize the supply side of the economy, while others focus on the demand side, but the true theory is one that puts equal emphasis on both sides. The policy implication of such a theory is that the government needs to create competition by breaking up oligopolies into smaller competing units. Let the invisible hand of Adam Smith become visible again. The government should enforce the antitrust laws that already exist. They have not been enforced since 1980. When Bill Clinton was president, 2,600 hundred mergers occurred in the oil industry alone. What was the need for Exxon and Mobil, two highly profitable companies, to become Exxon-Mobil? These companies were carved out of the split of Standard Oil in 1911, through the application of the Sherman Anti-Trust Act. Apparently, what was good in 1911, was no longer good in 1999.

Such is the extremely timely message of *New Macroeconomics*. It is a must read for anyone interested in comprehending what started the Great Recession of 2007, and why it still lingers in some insidious ways.

Dr. Ravi Batra
Southern Methodist University, Dallas, TX
October 3, 2017

Preface

According to the National Bureau of Economic Research (NBER), a deep recession started in the United States in December 2007 and ended in June 2009. However, most people recognize that even though the recession was said to be over, its aftereffects lingered well into the next decade, and even in 2017, some 10 years later, governments in America and around the world were struggling with problems of low growth, wage stagnation, and high poverty.

Economic policy became dramatically unconventional following the recession, which is now well known as The Great Recession, although some economists such as Professor Paul Krugman, a Nobel Laureate, called it a depression. Interest rates fell faster than ever before as almost all nations printed a lot of money. In the United States, the federal funds rate fell to nearly zero for more than 7 years, whereas the rates became negative in Europe and Japan. This was totally unheard of, and even in 2017, negative interest rates were common in these areas. Budget deficits also jumped enormously, all over the world.

Most economists were caught off guard, and they began to look for answers to something that had stunned them and kept them in shock for several years. They offered new theories, giving up old ideas, while some stuck to their past beliefs, and wished to do more of the same by raising government spending even faster. Thus, there has been a lot of tumult and turmoil within the economics profession, but it has produced a great by-product, which may be called "New Macroeconomics."

In the spirit of scientific inquiry, it is important to compare accepted theory with reality. Keynesianism remains the dominant paradigm in macroeconomics, and the 2008 meltdown revived Keynesian prescriptions. But the subsequent anemic and fraught recovery also intensified criticism of Keynesianism. This book examines consensus economics in the context of recent developments.

I confess that this book could be interpreted as a highly personal perspective. It draws upon ideas from a few well-known experts such as

Professors Joseph Stiglitz, Paul Krugman, and Ravi Batra, through the lens of my own experience in the technology sector. I do not aspire to give a balanced presentation of all viewpoints from economists belonging to every school of thought as it is just impossible for me to achieve that, but rather I present to the readers at large my own interpretation of where traditional macroeconomics does and doesn't explain facts on the ground. The final chapters of this book focus on the profound challenges and opportunities offered by technological progress.

New Macroeconomics is not the same thing as new classical economics or new Keynesian economics, both of which had been extensively analyzed by mainstream economists. Instead, it deals with subjects that mainstream economists had ignored until 2007. For instance, the question of growing inequality was never on the forefront of economic thought, but now it is, as both liberals and conservatives pay attention to the needs of a middle class that has been vanishing in America.

Similarly, the effects of environmental pollution, once totally ignored, are becoming a part of conventional economics. How the stock market interacts with macro policy is another hot topic among experts as well as policy makers. Above all, a revolutionary theory, known as the wage-gap theory, seems to have all the answers missing from traditional ideas. In fact, this wage-gap hypothesis formed a decent part of my first book entitled *Mass Capitalism: A Blueprint for Economic Revival.* In other words, new macroeconomics is totally new and has very little in common with conventional ideas of neoclassical and Keynesian economics.

Introduction

This chapter will include most ideas that were popular before the Great Recession. The neoclassical and Keynesian theories form the bulk of the material here and are described in an uncomplicated way that everyone can understand.

Global Economy in the New Millennium

Where the world stands today will be the subject of Chapter 2. The global economy has gone through a lot of churning. Why this happened and, in some ways, continues to happen will be examined here.

Macroeconomics of Income and Wealth Concentration

How income and wealth inequality affects an economy is discussed in Chapter 3. Here we begin with the views of Professors Stiglitz, Krugman, and Jeffrey Sachs—what they have in common and where they differ. The research of many others will also be discussed in detail because almost everyone agrees today that income and wealth disparities continue to rise even though economic growth has slowed around the world.

The Environment and Macroeconomics

How the changing environment and macro policy interact with each other are the ideas analyzed here. Pollution taxes and subsidies are being studied extensively nowadays. How they affect the macroeconomic performance is examined in Chapter 4. For instance, is a carbon tax better or worse than, say, an excise tax in terms of its effects on jobs, economic growth, and public well-being?

Stock Market and Macroeconomics

Stock ownership has grown substantially in the United States and globally. That is why central banks pay special attention to the effects of their policies on the stock market because its growth or crash can create a boom or a depression. However, many economists say that they do not understand how the stock market works, but new theories have emerged to answer their questions. Such theories are examined in Chapter 5.

The Wage-Productivity Gap

I believe the wage-gap theory answers all the questions that had been ignored by economists until 2007. I have studied this theory extensively and briefly analyzed it in my previous books *Mass Capitalism, Sustaining Moore's Law and How Information Revolution Remade the Business and the Economy*. But this time, I will discuss all its aspects, because this is a complete theory and includes the best ideas of both classical and Keynesian models. This theory makes the "New Macroeconomics" really new. Its policy implications are also different. It does not believe in constant application of Keynesian policies such as printing money or keeping a high budget deficit almost all the time. Instead, it follows the advice of Adam Smith, the father of modern economics, and advocates the presence of high competition among firms to make them efficient and be responsive to the needs of the consumer. Keynesian policies are needed in an emergency, but after the recession was declared over in 2009, they were no longer necessary. However, the U.S. federal debt continued to rise sharply and has not stopped rising. This shows that Keynesian policies are not as effective as they used to be, and the wage-gap theory says that monopoly capitalism or a system of oligopolies is the culprit. Hence, we need free-market *Mass Capitalism*.

The Wage-Gap and The Future of The Technological Sector

Chapter 7 deals with the future of the new technological sector and shows that this future is strongly connected to the wage-gap theory.

Summation

Finally, Chapter 8 summarizes the contents in all chapters of this book.

Acknowledgments

I owe my greatest intellectual debt to a great neohumanist, the Late Shri Prabhat Ranjan Sarkar, whose books have inspired me to keep writing about new ideas. Macroeconomics has changed in many ways since the start of the Great Recession, and this book is an attempt to offer this new look to the reader.

This venture would not have been possible without the encouragement that I received from the Managing Executive Editor of Business Expert Press, Scott Isenberg. It was Scott, who reminded me about putting my ideas into writing. I am also thankful to BEP's other editors, Dr. Philip Romero and Dr. Jeffrey Edwards. Both of them went through the manuscript carefully and offered many suggestions to improve my arguments and presentation of ideas.

Last but not least, I am very grateful to my mentor, Professor Ravi Batra. He guided me considerably through numerous discussions, read the manuscript carefully, and helped me present the arguments in a simple and reader-friendly way.

CHAPTER 1

Introduction

When John Maynard Keynes wrote his masterpiece, *The General Theory of Employment, Interest and Money*, in 1936, macroeconomics was dominated by a belief in laissez-faire, that is, the government should keep its hands off the economy. The subject of macroeconomics is quite old and we can find a discussion of what creates prosperity and a higher living standard in ideas offered as long ago as the third century BC. According to Navin Doshi, an engineer-cum-economist, economics, especially macroeconomics,

> has an ancient history. In the West, especially Greece, it was first propounded by the likes of Plato and Aristotle. In India, it was offered by Kautilya.
> *(Economics and Nature: Essays in Balance, Complementarity and Harmony,* p. 10)

Many economists regard Keynes as the most influential economist who founded modern macroeconomics. Yet, Kautilya, the author of *Arthshastra*, meaning the science of wealth, anticipated Keynes in many ways. Kautilya, the prime minister of a vast Mauryan empire, was a contemporary of Alexander the Great. He argued that the king should actively manage the economy and offer tax relief during bad economic times. In this way he anticipated what Keynes argued much later in his *General Theory*. I don't intend to downgrade Keynes' influence and contribution to economic thought. I just want to say that Keynes, who spent a few years as an officer of Her Majesty's Government in India, was not the first to offer ideas about fiscal policy.

In 1936, Keynes looked around and found a world in the middle of the worst depression in history. He wanted to do something about it, but conventional ideas stood in the way, because they were in favor of *laissez-faire*, which calls for no government intervention at all. However, Keynes persisted, met with several world leaders, and after World War II his theories were largely accepted by economists.

1.1   The Concept of Equilibrium

Keynes began with the concept of equilibrium in macroeconomics. Although equilibrium was a well-known concept in microeconomics, it had a special meaning in macroeconomics, which Keynes emphasized. In microeconomics, equilibrium generally refers to a balance between supply and demand for a certain product. For instance, the automobile market is said to be in equilibrium when demand for autos meets the supply, or the market for wheat is in equilibrium, when quantity of wheat demanded equals the quantity of wheat supplied.

Thus, in a single market, the concept of equilibrium is simple, but this is not the case in macroeconomics where we need to look at the economy as a whole, or all the markets in which consumers and producers are interested. The consumers generate demand and the producers generate supply. But how do we measure macro demand for consumption goods, because they are offered in different units. For example, the autos are described in terms of numbers, whereas wheat is described in terms of the bushels of production and consumption. The difficulty arises because how do we add apples to bananas and come up with an aggregate measure.

There is, however, a simple way to describe macro demand and supply. Macro demand, sometimes called aggregate demand, is in terms of money spent on various consumption and investment goods during a year; similarly, macro supply, also called aggregate supply, can be described as revenue or the money value of the production of these goods in 1 year. In theory, we look at the purchasing power of spending and business revenue, but in terms of practical economic policy, it is the money spent by consumers and investors and the money earned by producers that describe aggregate demand and supply.

Consumption goods are those that are in demand by consumers, and investment goods are those in demand by investors engaged in the process of production. Food, clothing, shelter, education, healthcare, and so on, are considered consumption goods and services, whereas office buildings, machines, and new homes are considered investment goods. So, the money spent on these goods is the major part of macro demand. But there are others who also spend money on such goods. For instance, the government at the federal and state levels buys such products too. So, government purchases are also included in aggregate demand. Foreigners also buy a nation's products. So, the value of exports is part of macro demand, but Americans spend money on foreign goods, so we need to subtract the value of imports from the total. Thus, aggregate demand (AD) may be written as:

AD = Consumer spending + Investment spending + Government spending + Exports – Imports.

Aggregate supply (AS), on the other hand, is the value of a nation's production of consumption and investment goods during a year, that is,

AS = Revenue of firms producing such goods.

AS is sometimes called gross domestic product (GDP), but it is measured by estimating aggregate spending on domestically produced goods.

When Keynes wrote his book, the government spending and tax revenues were relatively small; so, he initially ignored these items and began his analysis by noting that

AD = Consumption (C) + Investment (I)

Since all production becomes somebody's income, he wrote AS as,

AS = Aggregate income = Consumption (C) + Saving (S)

In order to understand this idea, let us see how we spend our income. It goes either into consumption or paying taxes, while the rest goes into savings. But since he started his analysis by assuming that tax revenue was unimportant, he wrote

$$AS = \text{Consumption} + \text{Saving}$$

In equilibrium, macro demand equals aggregate supply, or

$$\text{Consumption} + \text{Saving} = \text{Consumption} + \text{Investment}$$

And from this

$$\text{Saving} = \text{Investment}$$

in equilibrium. It should be clear by now that macro-equilibrium concept is different from the micro concept. When

$$AD = AS, \text{Saving} = \text{Investment}$$

This is how Keynes started his analysis.

In a global economy setting, where both foreign trade and the government sectors are prominent in almost all nations and should not be excluded from analysis, the concept of macro demand includes government spending and the trade deficit or surplus. In terms of symbols,

$$AD = C + I + G + X - M$$

where C is spending by consumers, I equals spending by investors, G is government spending, X stands for the value of exports, and M for the value of imports. Aggregate income now includes payment for taxes, so that

$$AS = GDP = \text{Aggregate Income} = C + S + T$$

where S stands for a nation's level of saving and T for its tax revenue. With AD = AS in equilibrium,

$$C + I + G + X - M = C + S + T,$$

which means that

$$I + G + X = S + T + M.$$

The left-hand side of this equation is usually described as injections, because each of its components is an addition to national spending, whereas the right-hand side is known as leakages, because its components are subtractions from the nation's spending. Thus, in macro equilibrium, when demand equals supply, leakages equal injections. It should be clear that macro equilibrium is more complex than micro equilibrium, where equilibrium simply means a balance between demand and supply and where the producer sells all its production. The micro concept is also valid in the macro area, but the macro economy also refers to some ideas not relevant in the micro setting.

1.2   A Balanced Economy

In a balanced economy, the equilibrium of a global economy becomes the same as the one Keynes first used. The concept of a balanced economy has been introduced by economist Professor Ravi Batra, who describes it as one where foreign trade and the budget deficit are in balance. Thus, when

$$X = M \text{ and } G = T,$$

so that the nation has no trade deficit and no budget deficit, then its economy is in balance. It should be clear from the leakage–injection equation that in a balanced economy X cancels out with M and G cancels out with T, so that

$$S = I.$$

Of course, there is hardly any nation today with a balanced economy. Most nations have massive ongoing budget deficits, while some have huge trade surpluses or deficits. Thus, the global economy faces vast imbalances that contribute to economic stagnation.

It should be noted that all these equilibrium concepts apply to almost all macro theories, including old as well as the new. Classical theories and Keynesian theories have at least this notion in common. They all use the same equilibrium conditions.

1.3   Classical Economics

Classical economics began when Adam Smith wrote his masterpiece, *An Enquiry into the Nature and Causes of the Wealth of Nations*. He did this in 1776, the same year when some colonies of America joined hands and declared independence from England. It turns out that the United States became a prosperous nation with the help of an economic system that Smith had described as ideal. So, it is more than a coincidence that Smith's book and American independence occurred in the same year.

Although Smith's book dealt mostly with micro concepts, he also touched upon some macro ideas that apply to the economy. He invented the idea of an invisible hand, which may be described as keen competition among firms in any industry. He assumed that people are generally self-interested and greedy, but this nature helps generate an efficient economy that raises economic growth and the general standard of living. For instance, facing keen competition from other firms, each producer has to offer high-quality products and sell them at reasonable prices to induce people to buy them. Otherwise a business loses customers and is stuck with unsold goods that generate losses. Thus, it is self-interest that makes a firm efficient.

Consumers too have a self-interest in buying high-quality goods at lowest prices, and this makes the companies efficient. Workers too have a self-interest in finding good jobs. They have to obtain the best training and work harder to earn a higher wage. Thus, self-interest or greed is good at all levels of the economy. We should not denounce greed, but we should denounce economic policies that reduce competition among businessmen, because without keen competition, firms will offer shoddy products and charge higher prices. People will generally suffer and the low level of competition will cause inflation that reduces real wages and hence the living standard. Thus, Smith criticized government policies that limited the number of firms in various industries.

Two quotes from Smith summarize his views. In the *Theory Of Moral Sentiments*, Smith wrote:

Every individual . . . neither intends to promote the public interest, nor knows how much he is promoting it . . . he intends only his own security; and by directing that industry in such a manner as its produce may be of the greatest value, he intends only his own gain, and he is in this, as in many other cases, led by an invisible hand to promote an end which was no part of his intention. (p. 184–85)

In his most famous book *The Wealth Of Nations*, Smith wrote:

It is not from the benevolence of the butcher, the brewer, or the baker, that we expect our dinner, but from their regard to their own interest. We address ourselves, not to their humanity but to their self-love, and never talk to them of our necessities but of their advantages. (p. 456)

During the 18th century, when Adam Smith wrote his book, religion had a strong influence on people's thinking. Self-interest and greed were not openly espoused because of the fear that they would create crime and anarchy. Smith's thought was revolutionary as he challenged conventional views that had prevailed since the sixth century, when the Catholic Church came to dominate people's thinking and lifestyle. But Smith argued that everyone's self-interest ensures that high-quality goods and services are produced at the lowest possible price, provided there is a strong competition among firms as well as workers. In this way, Smith denounced state monopolies and laborers' guilds that in those days restrained competition among businesses and employees.

According to Smith, the government should restrict its activity to national defense, law and order, and the provision of adequate infrastructure. In other words, the state should not engage in the management of the economy.

1.4   Development of Classical Economics

Smith laid the foundation of an economic framework that today is known as "classical economics," and after its popularity, some other writers developed it further in other areas. The most well-known among them was a French economist named Jean-Baptiste Say. He offered what we now know as Say's law of markets that asserts that supply creates its own demand. This is a simple statement but with far-reaching consequences. Normally, supply and demand are equal only in equilibrium, but according to Say's law they are always equal because when supply creates its own demand, a company is able to sell all its production, so that it remains profitable. Furthermore, the law argues that there are never layoffs, because layoffs occur only when a business has unsold goods, which are ruled out by the law.

In order to prove such a strong statement, Say assumed the existence of a barter economy where there is no money, and goods exchange for goods. Let us suppose that a family starts a furniture-producing business and builds chairs. Since there is no money in the economy, it can offer only chairs to buy goods from other families. It will then build enough chairs to meet its own needs of chairs and other goods. For instance, suppose it builds 100 chairs of which 10 chairs are for its own needs and the other 90 are exchanged for goods produced by other families. Thus, the family's total production of 100 chairs represents its total demand for all goods it needs. Thus, the family's supply equals its own demand. If the argument is extended to all the families, their supplies equal their demands. Thus, aggregate supply equals aggregate demand.

Say's law also argues that there is no need for the government intervention in the economy, because when supply equals demand, there are no layoffs or unemployment that might require the state's attention and intervention. Say thus made an argument for *laissez-faire*, that is, the government should never intervene in the economy.

1.5   The Rate of Interest

Subsequently, economists relaxed the strong assumption of a barter economy that has not prevailed for several centuries. They introduced a concept of the real rate of interest, which may be defined as (R), or

$$R = \text{Market interest rate} - \text{Rate of inflation}$$

They linked it to savings and investment. In Say's economy, there is little role for savings, which require the presence of money. In the absence of money, it is hard for a family to save money. And if there is no money, price inflation is likely to be absent. Thus, Say's law is not realistic, and subsequent writers tried to remove this flaw.

In a monetary economy that permits savings, supply is not always equal to demand, because savings are a leakage from spending or demand, and if they are high, consumer spending may not be enough to match the nation's supply. This creates the possibility of overproduction, recession, layoffs, and unemployment. However, classical economists argued that if the rate of interest is free to fall in a recession, then any layoffs are temporary and a free market system cures its problem of unemployment.

Money enables people to save but it also enables some others to borrow money and invest it to start or expand a business. People save money and deposit it with their banks, which in turn lend these savings to business people for investment. So, if investment spending equals these savings, then any fall in consumer demand is made up by investment so that total spending still equals the value of production. A simple example makes this point clear.

Suppose a nation's firms produce $500 worth of goods. Since all production becomes somebody's income, the nation's income also equals $500. If savings equal $100, then consumer spending is $400. But if these savings find their way into the hands of investors, then investment absorbs the unspent money and total spending equals $500. Thus, on the income side

$$\text{Nations' income} = \$500 = C + S = \$400 + 100 = GDP = \text{Aggregate Supply (AS)}$$

On the demand side,

$$\text{Aggregate Demand (AD)} = C + I = \$400 + \$100 = \$500$$

Thus, If $S = I = \$100$, there is no overproduction and hence no layoffs. This is how this chapter started, and this example illustrates the equilibrium concept further in a simple economy with small government and foreign trade, or in a balanced economy. It may be noted that the nation's income is not the same thing as the concept of national income that has a special meaning in modern macroeconomics. A nation's income is simply its gross domestic income, whereas national income is as follows:

National Income = GDP − depreciation − indirect business taxes + NFP,

where indirect business taxes are sales and excise taxes, depreciation is the wear and tear of capital stock, and NFP is a nation's net foreign income.[1]

What ensures that investment equals savings? This is where the self-interest of bankers comes in. The classical theory of the interest rate argues that if the real rate of interest rises, savings rise but investment falls. If the interest rate is above the equilibrium rate, then savings are high relative to investment, which results in overproduction and layoffs. If

$$S = \$100, \text{ but } I = \$80.$$

---

[1]There are more concepts in the GDP accounting system than presented in the main text. They are as follows:

GDP = The Value of a Nation's Output Produced at Home During a Year
NDP = GDP − Depreciation

Where depreciation is also called capital consumption. It is the wear and tear that capital or investment goods undergo in the process of producing other goods. In the United States, annual depreciation has been estimated to be 10 percent production.

Domestic Income = NDP − Indirect Business Taxes

Indirect business taxes represent the tax revenue that the government receives from sales and excise taxes.

National Income = Domestic Income + NFP

Where NFP stands for net factor payment from abroad or a nation's net foreign income. For instance, in the United States NFP equals the income of Americans from their asset holdings abroad minus the income of foreigners from their assets in America. For a balanced economy, NFP is fairly small, but when global imbalances are vast, NFP can be large enough to have a significant effect on national income. A trade-deficit nation such as the United States tends to have a negative NFP, whereas trade surplus nations such as China and Germany usually have a positive NFP.

there is overproduction of $20, because in a simple or balanced economy,

$$\text{Overproduction} = S - I.$$

Here the banks have idle funds worth $20, which affects their profits. In their self-interest, they lower the rate of interest and find more borrowers who thus borrow the remaining $20 and invest this money. Thus, investment goes back to the level of $100, and S = I. According to classical economists, this is a self-sustaining process, and the government does not have to tell the banks to lower their interest rate. The self-interest of bankers induces them to bring the interest rate down and thus get rid of their idle funds. So, now Say's law becomes: supply creates its own demand in the long run. In other words, in the short run, layoffs and unemployment are possible, but not in the long run, when the interest rate falls enough to eliminate layoffs.

1.6   The Role of the Real Wage

The question of employment has two aspects. First, layoffs should be avoided. Second, new entrants to the labor force should find jobs consistent with their qualifications. In other words, the economy or labor demand should grow fast enough to provide employment to the rising labor force. For this second aspect, the classical economists offered a theory of the labor market, which determines the real wage in equilibrium and also shows how jobs are provided to all those looking for work.

The real wage is the purchasing power of a nation's average salary, or how much this average salary buys. Classical economists argue that labor demand and labor supply are linked to the real wage. Again, it is a question of demand and supply with the real wage as labor price. If the wage rises, employers demand less labor, and if it falls, they want to hire more workers. On the supply side, a fall in the real wage is discouraging to workers, so some of them quit the labor market or work fewer hours. Either way, labor supply falls. Equilibrium in the labor market occurs when labor demand equals labor supply at a certain real wage. At this equilibrium, there is also full employment because all those willing to work at the prevailing wage have found jobs. This is how a competitive labor market generates employment for all workers.

Competition among workers is just as important as among firms. If there is unemployment, then some will accept lower wages that drive down the real wage. As the real wage falls, producers hire more workers until full employment is restored. Thus, as long as real wage is free to fall, full employment is assured. The classical theory of employment is now complete. Full employment occurs in the long run if the real wage and the real rate of interest are free to fall in case of unemployment. A flexible real wage ensures that labor demand is enough for the labor supply, whereas a flexible interest rate ensures that the output produced by these employees is sold out. Thus both the real wage and the interest rate have to be flexible to generate full employment. No government intervention is necessary as long as markets are competitive and prices are flexible. Thus, what Say stated for a barter economy also holds true for a monetary economy in the long run. Laissez-faire is all that a nation needs to stay prosperous.

1.7   Money Supply and Inflation

Classical economists also proposed a theory of inflation. For this they used the quantity theory of money, in which total spending equals the value of GDP. Their equation in this case is:

$$MV = PY$$

Here M is the money supply, V is the velocity of money, which is the number of times a dollar bill changes hands in a year, P is the average price, and Y is the nation's output. In this equation, MV is total spending and PY is GDP. Classical economists assume that V is constant, and using their theory of employment they argue that Y is constant in equilibrium, where a fully employed labor force produces a certain level of output. Since V and Y are both constant, it is clear that the average price level depends only on money supply. If the supply of money doubles, then the price level also doubles, and so on. This is the classical theory of inflation where the printing of extra money only raises prices and has no other effects.

1.8   Economic Policy

Classical economists offered a variety of theories regarding output, employment, the rate of interest, and inflation. All their theories had one objective which was to demonstrate that *laissez-faire* is the best economic policy. In practice, this policy made the following recommendations:

1. There should be no minimum wage because it restrains competition among unemployed workers.
2. There should be no labor unions because they also restrain worker competition.
3. There should be no other forms of government intervention, such as money printing or extra government spending to fight a recession, which is a short-run problem that goes away in the long run.
4. The government should balance its budget every year.

1.9   The Great Depression

Say's law, along with classical economics, remained popular for more than a century even though there were many recessions and even depressions where the unemployment rates would rise even above 15 percent. Some of these slumps lasted much longer than 2 years, which the classical economists had defined as the short run. But no scholar other than Karl Marx was able to challenge the attractive slogan of Say's law. But Marx's preference for communism destroyed his credibility and Say's law remained popular.

It was not before the Great Depression of the 1930s that classical economists faced a really serious challenge from Keynes who wrote a book in 1936. He argued that almost every classical theory was either wrong or illogical. He called for a massive government intervention to bring the economy out of depression, but no one took him seriously and the depression was ended in the 1940s by World War II.

1.10   Keynesian Economics

Keynes began by disproving Say's law that supply creates its own demand in the long run so that over time demand cannot be less than supply. He criticized the classical theory of the interest rate by pioneering a new idea that he called a consumption function. He said savings were not strongly linked to the interest rate; classical writers had argued that a rise in the interest rate leads to a rise in savings and hence a fall in consumption. Keynes argued that people's incomes, and not interest rates, were major determinants of their spending. If income rises, people spend more, and if income falls, they spend less. Savings also rise with income but only after a family has reached a minimum level of consumption.

These were radical ideas for those days, although today they are part of mainstream economics.

If savings and consumption are not related to the rates of interest, Say's law breaks apart. Keynes argued that if savings exceed investment then supply exceeds demand, leading to overproduction, recession, and layoffs. At this point, according to classical economists, the interest rate falls, leading to a fall in savings and a rise in consumption, until demand catches up with supply. This self-correcting mechanism could take about 2 years, so that in the long run demand rises to the level of supply. However, if savings and consumption do not respond well to the fall in the rates of interest, then demand may be short for a long time, and Say's law may not hold even in the long run. Keynes said something like this had been occurring during the 1930s, where investment opportunities were also limited, so that,

$$S > I \text{ and } AD < AS$$

for a very long time. Thus, the depression went on and on because demand remained well short of supply.

Keynes offered new theories in almost all area of macroeconomics. Here are some of his innovations:

$$C = SC + mpc.Y$$

where C is consumer spending, SC stands for subsistence consumption, and mpc is marginal propensity to consume, which is a positive fraction of new spending from a rise in income. The mpc is normally less than one. Suppose someone's income rises by $100 and of this $90 go into new spending, then

$$mpc = 90/100 = 0.9 \text{ or } 90\%$$

The remaining $10 go into savings, which gives rise to the concept of the marginal propensity to save, or

$$mps = 10/100 = 0.1 \text{ or } 10\%$$

The mps is the fraction of new income going into savings. Clearly,

$$mpc + mps = 1.$$

1.11   The Multiplier

Another interesting contribution from Keynes is the concept of the multiplier, which is a measure of how an initial change in spending affects output and employment. Suppose a businessman wants to expand his business and raises his investment by $100, this is the initial change in spending that raises demand by $100. The multiplier tells us that, if the economy is not at full employment or at its maximum potential, then GDP will rise by more than $100. This multiplier measures the effect of the initial change in spending on GDP, that is,

Multiplier = Change in GDP/Change in investment = $1/mps$

Since mps is a fraction, the multiplier exceeds one so that the change in GDP is larger than the change in investment. Thus, the initial change in spending has a magnified effect on output. However, there are some economists, such as Robert Barro and Milton Friedman, who argue that the multiplier for a rise in government spending is less than one. I will examine their arguments later in this chapter.

As spending rises by $100, demand also goes up by $100; producers then respond by raising the output by $100, which in turn raise incomes by $100. This may be called the first effect. As income rises, consumption rises in proportion to the mpc, which in turn further raises demand and hence output and income. This is then the second-round effect. Since mpc is a fraction, each round produces a smaller increase in demand, and ultimately this effect falls to zero. The total increase in output is then the sum of the output rise through all the rounds. This is how the rise in GDP exceeds the initial rise in spending. The multiplier formula is:

$$1/mps = 1/(1 - mpc)$$

Thus, a high value for mpc raises the size of the multiplier.

The multiplier adds an element of instability to the economy, especially when it contracts, as it did during the Great Depression. Keynes argued that there was a stock market crash in 1929, which led to a sharp fall in business confidence and investment. This initial fall in spending led to multiple falls in consumption through many rounds so that output kept falling through several quarters and a recession that began at the end of 1929 turned into a depression by 1931.

1.12   The Rate of Interest

Keynes offered a new theory of the interest rate because the classical theory was deficient in the sense that savings do not have a strong link with the interest rate. He said that the demand and supply for money determine the rate of interest in the money–market equilibrium. According to Keynes, the interest rate is the price of money, not of savings or investment. He argued that the money market is linked to the bond market and bond yield equals the rate of interest. If the interest rate rises, bonds become more attractive because of their higher yields and their demand goes up. So, people use their savings to buy more bonds, which means that money demand in the form of savings or checking accounts goes down. Thus, money demand has a negative link with the interest rate.

Money supply, on the other hand, is determined by the government and depends on government policy regarding this supply. When money demand equals money supply, there is equilibrium in the money market and the interest rate is determined. In this way, Keynes sought to show that the state has a policy instrument that can be used to direct the economy. By changing the supply of money, the government can act like banks, which, according to classical economists, bring down the interest rate to eliminate a recession and layoffs.

1.13   Keynes and the Classics

The macroeconomic view offered by the classical model is very different from that offered by Keynes. In the classical world, full employment and equilibrium go together. At a certain real wage, labor demand equals labor supply and full employment occurs. The output produced by this fully employed labor finds enough demand at a certain interest rate that is determined by the behavior of banks. This way a free market economy creates prosperity for everyone who wants to work. No government action is required to solve problems that do not exist. In fact, the government intervention makes matters worse and creates problems.

Keynes has a totally different view of how an economy works. In his view, output and employment are determined by aggregate demand and if demand is insufficient relative to the economy's maximum potential, then equilibrium occurs at less than full employment. Since unemployment is possible in equilibrium, it may exist for a long time, because markets in equilibrium do not change easily. No one then has an incentive to change their behavior. Only markets in disequilibrium move toward an equilibrium. This is what happened during the Great Depression, which began in 1929 and got worse because of the faulty policies offered by classical economics. The unemployment rate, which was around 3.5 percent at the start of 1929, went up sharply by the end of the year.

When the depression began, the classical economists, who advised the government, first told the public not to worry as they thought the situation would correct itself within 2 years. But by 1931, an underemployment equilibrium had occurred and it was not going to go away without government intervention to create jobs for the unemployed. However, the prevailing economic theory would simply not accept this idea because it would raise the budget deficit further. Tax revenue had already fallen sharply and raising the government spending further was not at all acceptable to the government's advisors. Instead, they recommended a sharp rise in tax rates so as to collect more revenue and lower the budget deficit. Tax rates more than doubled in 1932. According to Keynes, the tax rise was pure insanity, because it lowered disposable incomes and hence aggregate demand further. By 1934, the U.S. unemployment rate had risen to 25 percent, which was the highest rate ever.

In defense of classical economics, we may say that by the end of the 19th century, the United States had become perhaps the richest nation in the world under the guidance of classical theory. Recessions and depressions had indeed occurred in some decades, but each slump had corrected itself and was followed by an improved living standard. Furthermore, a sharp recession had occurred in 1921, just 8 years before 1929, but it went away within a year without any government intervention. Thus, the advice offered by conventional economists in the 1930s had a sound historical basis. In hindsight, Keynes turned out to be right, but hindsight is 20–20. Even Keynes did not call for government intervention during the sharp recession of 1921.

1.14   Keynesian Economic Policies

Keynes offered a variety of economic policies that were designed to end the depression. They were of two types, depending on the type of disequilibrium.

1. If the economy is at full employment equilibrium, the state should not do anything. *Laissez-faire* is fine at this point.
2. If there is unemployment, then the state should bring about an increase in aggregate spending by means of fiscal and monetary policies.
3. If aggregate demand is larger than full employment output and prices rise fast, then the state should do the opposite, that is, bring demand under control by means of monetary and fiscal policies.

Fiscal policies deal with the government budget or surplus. During a slump, the deficit should be raised, and this can be done in two ways. Either raise government spending or cut tax rates or do both. A rise in government spending through increased borrowing directly raises spending in the economy, whereas a tax cut raises peoples' disposable income and their spending. In both cases aggregate spending rises and raises output manifold through the process of the multiplier. As output increases, those laid off are called back to work, and unemployment declines. Keynes called this process expansionary fiscal policy.

Monetary policies deal with the supply of money. This policy should also be expansionary so as to bring down the rate of interest, which will then raise investment spending and then demand. The effect is similar to that of fiscal expansion. However, monetary expansion does not work if the economy is in a depression, because then demand for bond is extremely high and bond prices have risen so much that interest rates hit bottom and cannot go down any further. Since the interest rate cannot go down any further, monetary expansion becomes ineffective. Keynes calls this the case of a liquidity trap. At this point only fiscal expansion works. Keynes thus preferred fiscal expansion to monetary expansion, especially when the fiscal case works immediately, whereas monetary policy works only after a lag.

If an economy faces high inflation that normally arises when demand exceeds full employment output, both the budget deficit and money supply should be reduced by the government. Here then both fiscal and monetary policies are contractionary. Thus, Keynes offers a variety of policies that the government may follow, depending on the state of disequilibrium. When there is no disequilibrium, then the government should not intervene.

Keynes has been often accused of recommending fiscal irresponsibility. This is not true, because he called for budget deficits only in a recession or depression. Once the economy recovers and full employment returns, there should be a budget surplus. He recommended balancing the budget over the business cycle that normally extends over 5 years. He was against balancing the budget every year, because this policy requires raising tax rates in a recession when the tax revenue falls because of a contracting economy, and makes things worse.

Keynes also argued in favor of state activism because of capitalism's tendency to have high-income inequality that tends to increase savings and lower aggregate demand. The mps of the rich is larger than the mps of the poor. So, the rich save far more than the poor, and savings tend to rise when inequality grows. Low consumption spending resulting from high savings in turn raises unemployment and poverty.

Keynes wrote his book in 1936 and even though he had found many logical flaws in classical economics, his message was completely ignored. Even as late as 1939, according to the *Historical Statistics of the United States*, the US unemployment rate exceeded 17 percent. However, that year Hitler started World War II, and the United States took the side of allied powers that included England and France among others. They needed arms, food grains and many other materials. US government spending went up sharply to buy these things and export them at no charge to the allies. The spending kept increasing as the allies suffered one defeat after another. In 1941, the United States also entered the war, following the Japanese invasion of Pearl Harbor. The budget deficit shot up and the multiplier process kicked in. Both the output and employment began to rise and by 1942, the unemployment rate returned to the level of 1929—around 3.5 percent.

The economics profession realized that budget deficits were not bad after all. Keynes was vindicated and his ideas gained popularity as the depression ended swiftly. He became a hero, but he died soon after the war ended in 1945. Keynesian economics replaced classical economics and new types of policies were devised.

1.15   Automatic Stabilizers

The first policy change occurred in the form of automatic stabilizers. Economists discovered that in order to minimize the fluctuations in employment, aggregate demand must be stabilized. An automatic stabilizer is an instrument that creates such stability. There are two main stabilizers: the progressive income and unemployment compensation. Due to the progressive nature of the income tax, whenever the economy contracts and incomes fall, the income tax rate also falls so that the after-tax income falls by less; this puts a cushion under the falling aggregate demand. Secondly, some workers are laid off but they are entitled to unemployment compensation for 6 months during which they receive up to 60 percent of their wage. This is the law in the United States, whereas in Europe unemployment benefits are more generous. Thus, unemployment compensation also restrains the fall in spending. The demand cushion comes into play automatically because of the stabilizers without new legislation.

The stabilizers also work when the economy is in boom and inflation threatens because of soaring spending. As economic growth picks up and incomes rise, the income tax rate also rises so that the after-tax income does not rise fast, which puts a cap on the rise in consumer spending; unemployment compensation also declines. Thus, automatic stabilizers work to control both inflationary and deflationary pressures.

1.16   Post-Keynesian Economics

Keynes passed away in 1946 and the evolution of macroeconomics since then may be termed "post-Keynesian economics." The automatic stabilizers dampened the fluctuations in aggregate demand, but they seemed to create a new problem that had never affected the American economy in the past, where prices were more or less stable. From 1820 to 1940, for instance, the consumer price index (CPI) had remained constant. There were indeed strong fluctuations in CPI, especially during the Civil War decade of the 1860s and the World War I decade of the 1910s. Prices went up sharply in those decades, but after the end of these wars, CPI declined sharply. For the entire time period 1820–1940, CPI was more or less constant. Ever since 1940, however, CPI has been generally rising, except for 1 or 2 years. This is something totally new and Keynes had not addressed this problem. The model that his followers developed to explain persistent inflation is known as the neo-Keynesian model.

Neo-Keynesian models generally assume a global economy where equilibrium occurs when

$$S + T + M = I + G + X$$

Keynes implicitly assumed that the nation's price level is more or less constant until full employment, but the neo-Keynesian model assumes it to vary with economic conditions. The model then shows that AD has a negative link with the price level (P), whereas AS is positively related to P in the short run but has no relationship in the long run. In other words, if P rises, AD falls and short-run AS rises. In the long run, the AD relationship does not change, but the one between AS and P does. Here then AS is constant regardless of the price level.

A rise in aggregate demand through monetary and fiscal expansion still raises output and employment in a recession but less than the case where the price level is constant.

The neo-Keynesian analysis makes two main points. First, it shows that prices may rise because of expansionary policies even before recession ends, which is what has been happening in the world since the end of World War II. Second, expansionary policies are not as effective as Keynes believed. In other words, a higher budget deficit is needed to reach full employment, or a larger monetary expansion is needed to do the same. Both tendencies tend to explain why prices keep rising year after year.

A constant rise in prices year after year is a new problem for the economy, but the neo-Keynesians do not consider it a problem as long as the annual rate of inflation is reasonable and no larger than 2 percent. This belief comes from their theory of the Phillips curve, which asserts that there is a trade-off between inflation and unemployment. Low unemployment rates are associated with higher rates of inflation. This theory became popular during the 1950s and is associated with the name of an economist from New Zealand, A.W. Phillips.

At first, like Keynes, the neo-Keynesians preferred fiscal expansion to monetary expansion in fighting unemployment even though their model shows that larger budget deficits are required to achieve full employment when prices go up. But since unemployment is a bigger evil than inflation, they assert that we should live with constant inflation.

1.17 Monetarism

The neo-Keynesian analysis had its critics who argued that inflation can easily get out of control if the budget deficit keeps rising. The most prominent critic was Milton Friedman, who went on to win a Nobel prize for his critique. He criticized Keynes for being wrong on many points. His school of thought is known as monetarism because he claimed that money supply is the major determinant of economic activity. He advocated the classical policy of *laissez-faire* and the avoidance of government intervention in the economy except in an emergency situation like the Great Depression.

The state intervention, according to Friedman, should have been in the form of monetary expansion and not fiscal expansion to raise the budget deficit. He based this argument on crowding out, which asserts that a rise in the budget deficit increases government borrowing to pay for the deficit. Since the government is a large borrower, there is a rise in loan demand and the interest rate goes up, which in turn lowers the level of investment. This way increased government spending crowds out investment and makes the fiscal policy ineffective. If the budget deficit rises and investment falls at the same time, aggregate demand may or may not rise. So fiscal policy becomes ineffective. Because of crowding out, Friedman prefers monetary expansion to fiscal expansion in an emergency situation like the Great Depression. The fiscal expansion multiplier may become less than one because of crowding out.

The neo-Keynesians accepted the crowding-out argument and revised their theory. If the government does not borrow money to pay for increased spending but just prints it, then the interest rate will not rise from fiscal expansion and crowding out will be avoided. Thus, fiscal expansion will remain effective to maintain full employment. Printing money to pay for a deficit rise is known as deficit financing, which has been the preferred method of neo-Keynesians to fight unemployment.

1.18   Rational Expectations

Friedman found it hard to believe that the neo-Keynesians would ignore the threat of high inflation appearing from the policy of deficit financing. He then offered a money growth rule that is consistent with price stability. Using the classical quantity theory of money that

$$MV = PY$$

where once again M is money supply, V is money's velocity, P is the price level, and Y is output, he argued that since V is constant and Y is constant at full employment in the classical model, P remains constant if

$$\text{Money growth} = \text{Output growth}$$

This was Friedman's money growth model to maintain stable prices. In the long run, American output has grown about 3.5 percent per year.

Friedman's argument is that money growth per year should approximate this level. He also warned that breaking this rule leads to high inflation in the long run, and raises the real rate of interest to generate a recession and high unemployment. This defeats the very purpose of fiscal expansion.

Another school of thought emphasized the role of rational expectations and argued that when prices rise year after year because of deficit financing, rational people including workers come to believe that fiscal expansion is always inflationary. Whenever the government announces that deficit financing is going to rise, they anticipate higher inflation and immediately ask the employer to raise their wages in proportion to the expected rate of inflation. As wages rise, the cost of production also rises, and the employer has to raise prices to remain profitable. This way inflation may get out of control without curing unemployment and recession.

Friedman agreed with neo-Keynesians that fiscal expansion could eliminate a recession and unemployment in the short run, but he argued that in the long run things get worse and then the recession returns with greater strength. But according to the rational expectations argument, there is no benefit from deficit financing even in the short run, because workers demand an immediate rise in wages in proportion to expected rise in inflation. This school is purely classical and believes in *laissez-faire* to avoid any government intervention in the economy. That is why this school is called "neo-classical." It is simply old wine in a new bottle.

1.19   Supply-Side Economics

During the 1960s and the 1970s, the policy of deficit financing was followed to keep employment high. By 1979, inflation was out of control as the annual rate of inflation approached 14 percent. With prices rising by more than 1 percent per month, the rate of interest rose sharply and caused the worst recession since the 1930s. Neo-Keynesian critics had predicted all this, but their warnings had been ignored by policy makers. A new idea now emerged offered by an economist named Arthur Laffer. He argued that high-income tax rates, not deficit financing, were the real problem. He suggested that such rates should be cut sharply for individuals and corporations to raise savings, investment, and economic growth. This would also reduce the budget deficit as high output growth would generate such large rise in incomes that the tax revenue would actually rise to cut the budget deficit. Laffer called his tax cuts as supply-side economics as opposed to the neo-Keynesian policy of demand-side economics.

Laffer's theories were sharply criticized at that time, especially his idea that the budget deficit would fall after the sharp tax cuts, but the new president, Ronald Reagan, accepted his ideas, and thus income along with corporate tax rates were cut sharply in June 1981.

Not surprisingly, the budget deficit jumped even before the tax cuts went into effect, because the Federal Reserve chairman Paul Volcker adopted a policy of monetary contraction to bring inflation under control. Interest rates were already very high and went up further. The economy had started to contract in 1979, but in 1981, it went into a full-fledged contraction, with the unemployment rate jumping to 10 percent.

The budget deficit also went out of control because of those automatic stabilizers and the recession; finally, tax rates were raised but in a different form. All tax rates except the income taxes went up sharply in 1983, which meant that the supply-side economics had failed. However, inflation fell fast and Volcker quickly cut interest rates, and the economy began to recover. President Reagan became popular again and so did the supply-side economics.

Since then the supply-side economics has prevailed and because of its tolerance for budget deficits the federal debt reached an all-time high in 2017.

Summary

This chapter presents a brief account of various schools of thought of macroeconomics. By and large, there are two schools—the interventionist and *laissez-faire*. Until about 1940, the *laissez-faire* school dominated economic policy, but after World War II, the interventionist school overpowered became dominant. Since 2007, when the Great Recession started, the interventionist thought has become stronger even in the academic circles. But there are new theories as well, which we will study in the upcoming chapters.

Bibliography

Batra, Ravi. *Common Sense Macroeconomics*. Liberty Press, Texas, 2003. (Second edition published in 2012.)

Batra, Ravi. *End Unemployment Now: How to Eliminate Joblessness, Debt and Poverty Despite Congress*. Palgrave Macmillan, New York, 2015.

Blanchard, Olivier. *Macroeconomics Updated (5th ed.)*. Prentice Hall, Englewood Cliffs, 2011.

Cohn, Steven Mark. *Reintroducing Macroeconomics: A Critical Approach: A Critical Approach*. Taylor & Francis, 2015, p. 111.

Davis, William L., Figgins, Bob, Hedengren, David, Klein, Daniel B. "Economic Professors' Favorite Economic Thinkers, Journals, and Blogs" *Econ Journal Watch*. 2011; 8(2):126–146.

de Rugy, Veronique, Debnam, Jakina R. "Does Government Spending Stimulate Economies?", July 14, 2010. https://www.mercatus.org/publication/does -government-spending-stimulate-economies

Doshi, Navin. *Economics and Nature: Essays in Balance, Complementarity and Harmony*. Nalanda International, Los Angeles, 2012.

Forder, James. *Macroeconomics and the Phillips Curve Myth*. OUP, Oxford, 2014.

Friedman, Milton. *Capitalism and Freedom*. The University of Chicago Press, Chicago, 40th anniversary edition, 2002.

Keynes, John Maynard. *The General Theory of Employment, Interest and Money*. Penguin, London, 2015.

Laffer, Arthur B. *The End of Prosperity: How Higher Taxes Will Doom the Economy—If We Let It Happen*. Threshold Editions, New York, 2009.

Mankiw, N. Gregory. *Principles of Economics*. Cengage Learning, 2014.

Marx, Karl. *Das Kapital: A Critique of Political Economy*. Progress Publishers, Moscow, USSR. 1887.

Mishkin, Frederic S. *The Economics of Money, Banking, and Financial Markets*. Addison-Wesley, Boston, 2004, p. 517.

Say, Jean-Baptiste. *A Treatise on Political Economy; or the Production, Distribution or Consumption of WEALTH*. Translated from the Fourth edition of the French by C.R. Prinsep. 1821.

Smith, Adam. *An Enquiry into the Nature and Causes of the Wealth of Nations*. 9 March 1776.

Smith, Adam. *The Theory of Moral Sentiments*. 6th edition. A. Millar Publications, London, 1790.

Solow, Robert. "Neoclassical Growth Model". In Snowdon, Brian; Vane, Howard. *An Encyclopedia of Macroeconomics*. Edward Elgar Publishing, Northampton, 2002.

CHAPTER 2

Global Economy in the New Millennium

The Great Recession began at the end of 2007, but its causes were hidden in what had happened at the start of the new millennium. The chairman of the Federal Reserve in 2000 was Alan Greenspan, whose first term began in 1987, the year of the greatest stock market crash in history. Share prices fell more than 21 percent on October 19, 1987, almost double the level of a single-day fall in the Dow Jones Index in October 1929. Greenspan acted with great speed, increased the supply of money, and cut interest rates sharply soon after the 1987 crash. With more money available to banks and brokerages, share prices stabilized within a few months, and the economy began to grow again.

Greenspan learned an important lesson from this experience. Share prices crashed again in 2000 at the start of the new millennium. Greenspan cut interest rates again. Then came the massacre of 9/11 and the shaky stock markets fell more, and Greenspan cut rates one more time. So, in the new millennium the rate of interest fell repeatedly. This was bound to have unexpected consequences in markets that benefit from low interest rates.

2.1   The Housing Bubble

A nation's central bank normally lowers interest rates by cutting the federal funds rate, which is a fee that a bank charges another bank for overnight loans. The central bank does this by supplying extra funds to banks. In 2001, Greenspan lowered the federal funds rate, and did this again in 2002. The rate fell from 6.5 percent in 2001 to just 1 percent in 2002. This was a drastic and unprecedented fall.

The housing market is usually the first to react to lowering of rates. Homes are expensive and the vast majority of people buy them through borrowed money. The fall in the federal funds rate caused a big fall in the mortgage rate, so that home buyers could get money cheaply and afford to buy new homes. Demand for homes rose and with money available at very low rates, it kept rising year after year. Mortgage rates also declined in other countries and demand for homes rose all over the world.

As demand for homes rose, home prices began to rise, and as interest rates remained low for a long time, both demand for homes and prices rose year after year. When the price of something rises so swiftly and for so long, it is said to produce a bubble, especially when people start speculating in it. With home prices rising again and again, speculators moved into this market. Speculators bought homes either to rent them or sell them quickly at a profit. When one speculator made quick money, others also came in to make quick profit. This way the demand for homes kept rising from the actions of those who bought homes as their residence and others who bought them for speculation. So, the housing bubble continued to expand for many years. The bubble started in 2001, and it kept on going until the middle of 2006.

Money lenders benefitted a lot from the housing bubble. With money available cheaply from the Federal Reserve, banks loaned it out to home buyers and speculators. They earned huge fees for themselves and great profits for the speculators. Easy money also made the bankers take unusually large risks. They loaned out vast amounts to the public through home equity loans. People mortgaged their old homes, borrowed money, and spent it freely. Some banks also acted with fraud. They did not care if the borrower had good credit or had enough assets to repay the loan. All they wanted was to earn a fat fee from the loan. In some cases, the loan amount was more than the market value of the house because the bigger the loan, the greater the fee earned by a banker.

By the middle of 2007, the home market had reached its saturation; home prices had risen so much that demand for homes began to fall. That is when the housing bubble began to pop. At first the pop was slow, but as expectations were suddenly reversed the bubble popped more. So, the housing market crashed by the end of 2007.

The economy had benefitted a lot from low interest rates, as home production rose in response to rising demand for homes. Demand for automobiles and other expensive items usually bought on credit had also risen sharply because of very low interest rates, and unemployment had fallen to about 4 percent by 2007. But when the housing market crashed, things began to move in the opposite direction.

First, some workers were laid off in the housing industry and since some of these workers had bought homes at inflated prices, they could not pay their monthly mortgage to their banks. The housing crisis began to spread and gradually became the banking crisis. Layoffs began to expand from one industry to another. As more people were fired from their jobs, they could not service their automobile loans. Millions of people had bought cars on zero percent financing by making no down payment. The multiplier process began working in the negative direction, and layoffs kept spreading.

By the middle of 2008, several financial firms were under pressure and were facing bankruptcies. Bear Sterns, AIG, Merrill Lynch, Lehman Brothers, among many others, were on the verge of default on their own loans. Even the government-based organizations such as Fannie May and Freddie Mac faced trouble from bad mortgage loans that they had made to millions of home buyers. The debt supported economic system began to collapse. It was clear that this was not an ordinary recession.

The government moved quickly to bail out the financial institutions. Even very large institutions such as AIG and Merrill Lynch were bailed out with federal money. The Federal Reserve also bailed many banks out. Still thousands of people were laid off every month. General Motors and Chrysler declared bankruptcy and were bailed out. The rate of unemployment, which was around 4.5 percent in 2007, rose past 6 percent in 2008 and past 10 percent in 2009, which was the year when the recession was declared over. In fact, unemployment kept rising in 2010 as well. Normally, economic recovery comes after a recession, but this time it did not show itself. The layoffs continued even when output stopped failing.

The budget deficit rose, and continued to rise. The Federal Reserve also kept printing money to bring down the federal funds rate and the discount rate. The discount rate is the interest rate that a central bank charges for its loans to commercial banks. By 2010, the discount rate fell from 5 percent in 2007 to just 1 percent and the federal funds rate from 6 percent to 0.05 percent. Financial institutions could now borrow money at practically no cost from the Federal Reserve, something that had not occurred since the Great Depression.

All these were Keynesian and neo-Keynesian policies, and while they had been quite effective in prior recessions, this time around they were too slow to have much positive impact. Indeed, they stabilized the economic system eventually but created huge waste for the entire system.

Supply-side economic policies that had been put in practice in the 1980s were still prevalent. President Reagan had endorsed these policies and despite his promises to bring down the budget deficit, the deficit had stayed high throughout his 8 years. President George Bush Jr. and Vice President Dick Cheney were in charge in 2007 and 2008, and they continued what President Reagan had started. In fact, Dick Cheney once said that Reagan showed deficits didn't matter. They seemed to matter a lot during the Great Recession because the government spent trillions of dollars by 2014, and yet total employment was no higher than its level in 2007, as shown in Figure 2.1.

Where did all this money go? This is a question that will be answered in subsequent chapters of this book. For now, we just raise this question before the government wishes to increase its spending further.

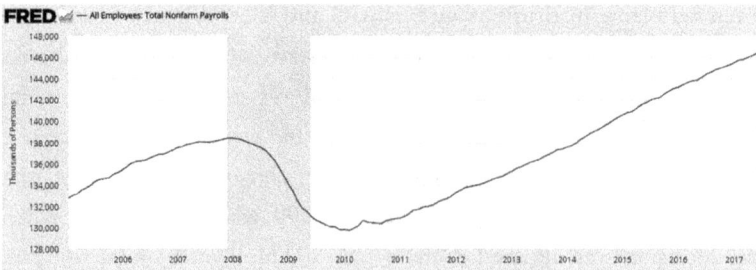

Figure 2.1 Nonfarm employment between 2005 and 2017 (in thousands)

Source: This graph is a reproduction from Federal Reserve Economic Data and has no title in the original. It shows that nonfarm employment in 2014 was essentially the same as in 2008 and has been increasing steadily rising since 2010 till date (https://fred.stlouisfed.org/series/NPPTTL).

2.2   The Rest of the World

The Great Recession started in the United States with the collapse of the housing market, but it quickly spread to the rest of the world, especially Europe and Japan. It looks like the same type of macroeconomics is taught all over the world. Central bank policies are also the same everywhere. Interest rates fell sharply in most countries after the recession became worse in the United States. Some other nations had experienced a stronger speculation boom in housing, especially Britain and Australia.

Once housing collapsed in America, it collapsed in other countries too. The unemployment rate in Eurozone had reached a low of 7 percent in 2008, but it jumped to 10 percent in 2010. This was also the year in which unemployment peaked in the United States, but in Europe it kept rising and reached a high level of 12 percent in 2013.

In some nations such as Greece and Spain, unemployment rates were as high as those in the Great Depression. Asian nations such as Japan and South Korea also suffered a great deal with output falling and unemployment rising. Both nations have large trade surpluses with America and as the American economy fell sharply, their exports also fell a lot. BRIC nations that include Brazil, Russia, India, and China also suffered, although economic growth did not become negative in India and China. But Russia and Brazil experienced a fall in output and a rise in unemployment.

2.3   Most Nations Print Money

Economic policy around the world was similar to that followed in the United States. Every economically advanced nation cut interest rates sharply by printing a lot of money. Nowadays money supply rises in two steps, one by printing extra money and two by the central bank writing more checks to other banks. There is also another way that money supply rises. When the central bank buys government bonds in the bond market from other banks and writes more checks to them, they get more cash from the central bank. This also raises their money supply.

After 2008 central banks bought not only more government bonds but also bonds from other financial institutions. For example, the Federal Reserve bought mortgage bonds from some financial institutions in addition to bonds from the federal government. The effect of these practices is the same as that of printing money. Thus, most nations printed tons of money to fight rising unemployment. The chairman of the Federal Reserve at the time was Dr. Ben Bernanke. He came to be known as 'Helicopter Ben' for his alleged remark that he would drop money from a helicopter if it became necessary to stabilize the economy. And his monetary policy appears to show that he faithfully followed his words.

In the United States, interest rates fell nearly to zero, but in some other nations, they even became negative. Japan and Europe had negative interest rates after 2012. Negative rates had never existed before. When Keynes criticized classical economics, his argument was that it would require negative interest rates to bring savings down to the level of investment, and that he argued was very unlikely. If savings exceeded investment then aggregate demand would remain less than the economy's potential output and that full employment would not return. Keynes must be very disturbed in his grave to see what his followers have done to his economic advice of balancing the budget deficit over the business cycle, but not every year. Hardly anyone bothers about balancing the budget anymore.

The 5-year German government bond had a negative yield of –0.2 percent in June 2017 compared to more than 1.8 percent in the United States. In Japan, the 5-year bond also had a negative yield. This means that a bond-buyer in Germany and Japan loaned money to the government and also paid it some money for safekeeping. All this reflects the vast amounts of euros the European Central Bank (ECB) had printed since the start of the Great Recession; similarly, the government of Japan had also printed huge amounts of yen.

Who knows why they had followed such policies? The results were not very encouraging. They had a goal of achieving a 2 percent rate of inflation as if inflation is very desirable. Their beliefs in the Phillips curve were as strong as ever, even though the hypothesis of inflation-unemployment trade-off had badly failed in the late 1970s. This is certain to disturb Milton Friedman in his grave. Friedman had criticized these policies sharply during the 1970s, when it was clear that high money growth had resulted in double-digit inflation. His advice that money growth should not exceed GDP growth was totally ignored. In June 2017, the unemployment rate in Eurozone was still above 9 percent compared to

7 percent in 2008. Almost a decade had passed and after printing trillions of euros, this is all that easy money policy had achieved.

The Federal Reserve began to realize in 2015 that rates had been low long enough. They then started raising the federal funds rate by 0.25 percent about every 6 months. By the middle of 2017, they had raised the rate to 1.25 percent. They also announced that they were going to reduce their bond holdings of about $4.5 trillion, which was below one trillion in 2007.

2.4   Most Nations Have a Huge Budget Deficit

According to the Economic Report of the President issued in 2017, the U.S. federal deficit was $342 billion in 2007; it almost doubled in 2008 and peaked in 2009 at more than $1.5 trillion. After that it remained above $1 trillion until 2012 and then slowly declined in coming years. Even in 2013, the level of employment was below that in 2007. What an irony? Trillions of dollars were spent by the government just to show that employment was still below the level 6 years before.

In percentage terms, the situation looked even worse. In 2007, the deficit as a percentage of GDP was about 1 percent; it jumped to 3 percent in 2008 and peaked at 10 percent in 2009. Even in 2013, when employment had caught up with that prior to the recession, the deficit was 4 times the level in 2007. In 2017, it was still more than double the level in 2007. The main point is that the policy of fiscal expansion is subject to diminishing returns. As a result, the US public debt jumped manifold as shown in Figures 2.2 and 2.3.

Budget deficits and debts in other nations also jumped, as is clear from Figure 2.4. The Euro government deficit peaked at 6 percent of Eurozone GDP in 2010 and Germany's deficit peaked at 4 percent. Since then the deficits have declined while Germany had a surplus in 2016 and 2017. The German economy has performed the best in Europe, which shows that prosperity does not depend on high deficits.

Japan has had high budget deficits since 1990 when its stock market crashed. The Nikkei index reached its peak at around 40,000 and even after several decades of money printing and high budget deficits, the index moves around 20,000. Japan has been the most prominent in following

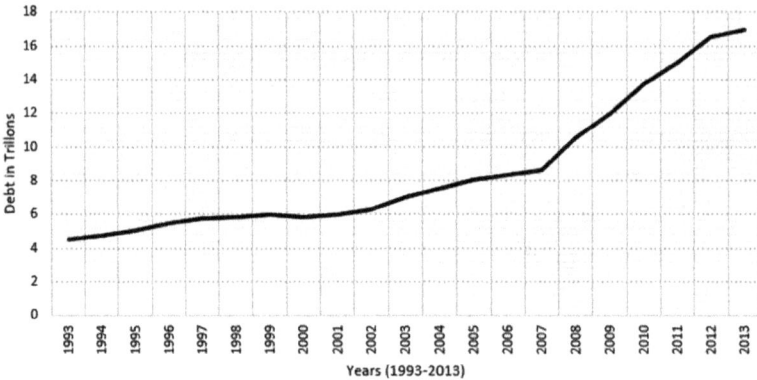

Figure 2.2 US public debt (1993–2013)

Source: Bjonnes, Roar, Hargreaves, Caroline. *Growing A New Economy*. Figure 15, p. 32. Other Sources: Bureau of Public Debt, United States Department of Treasury.

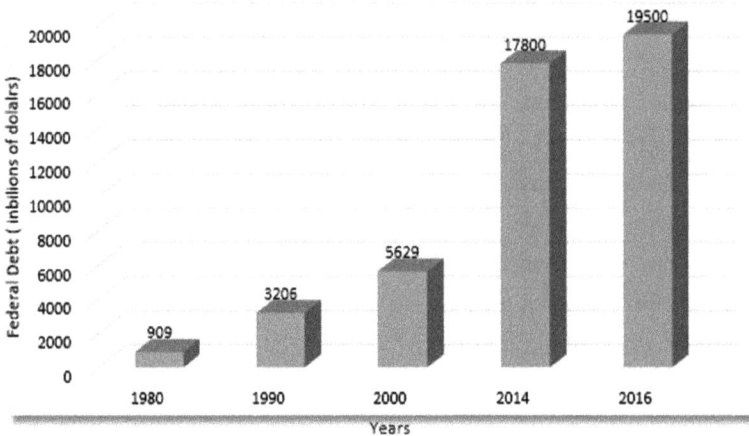

Figure 2.3 Federal debt (1980–2016)

Source: Batra, Ravi. *End Unemployment Now*. p. 21. Other Source: Council of Economic Advisers, The Economic Report of the President, 2017.

Keynesian policies. Please remember that these policies are not policies of Keynes but those of his followers. They are also what supply-side econo-mists like, namely record budget deficits along with low income tax rates but high taxes on other items such as high sales and excise taxes.

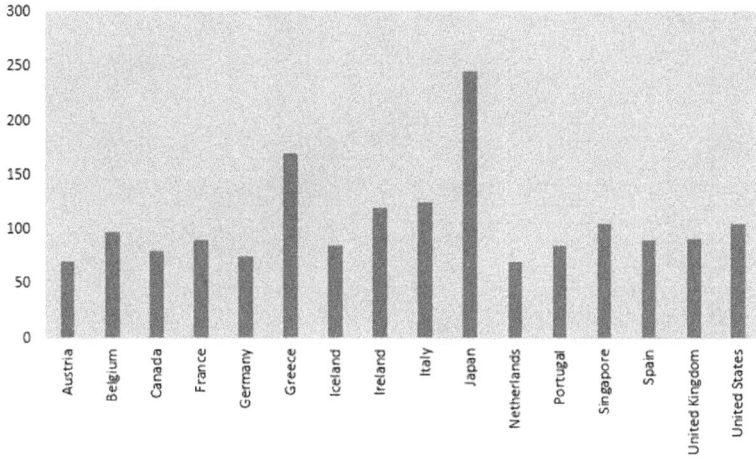

Figure 2.4 Government debt as % of GDP (2013)

Source: Bjonnes, Roar, Hargreaves, Caroline. *Growing A New Economy*. Figure 14, p. 31. Other Sources: World Bank Economic Outlook Database April 2013.

Japan's budget deficit peaked at 9.5 percent of GDP in 2009 and has steadily declined since then. In 2017, it was at 4.5 percent, but its unemployment rate is the lowest among advanced economies, at less than 3 percent in 2017. However, some economists say this rate is low because of its shrinking labor force.

2.5   Most Nations Have Stagnant Wages

It is well known by now that the real wage has stagnated in the United States ever since 1981 when supply-side economics took over. But it has also stagnated in most other countries. According to the 2017 Economic Report of the President, the real wage of production workers in 1980 was at 291, fell to 284 by 2000, and then recovered to 291 by 2007. Between 1980 and 2007, there was no improvement in the real wage as shown in Figure 2.5. The production workers are also called non-supervisory workers while others are known as supervisory workers. Since there are relatively few supervisors in any factory, production and non-supervisory workers constitute a large fraction of the labor force. According to the Economic Report of the President (2017), "These groups account for

Index, 1947=100 (log scale)

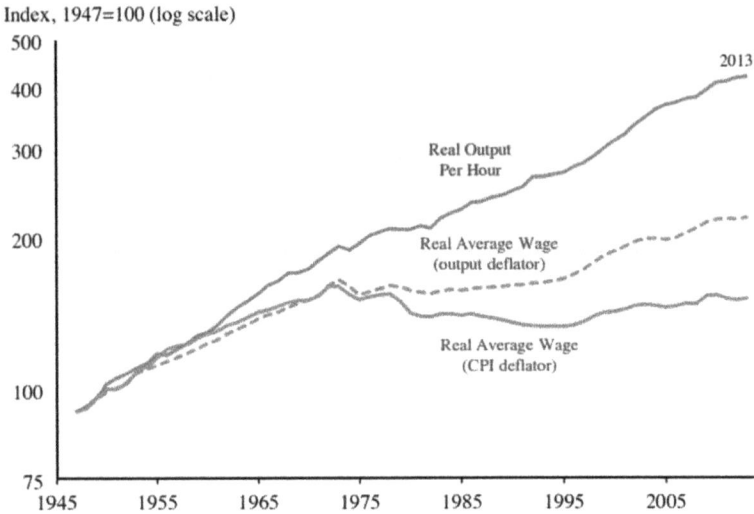

Figure 2.5 *Growth in productivity and average wage (1947–2013)*

Source: Council of Economic Advisers, The Economic Report of the President, 2014.

four-fifths of the total employment on private nonfarm payrolls" (p. 582, Table B-15). Thus, for a very large number of Americans, wages had been constant while their biggest tax burden coming from the social security tax and the sales tax had risen sharply.

Finally, the huge budget deficit and money printing had something positive to show, because by 2015 the real wage had risen to 305. In the meanwhile, the real per-capita GDP had risen from about 28,000 in 1980 to about 52,000 in 2017, which was a rise of 86 percent. Thus, while the real wage went up by 5 percent, the nation's productivity, which some say is represented by real per-capita GDP, had gone up by 86 percent. This is clearly wage stagnation. The workers should be thankful to the vast rise in the budget deficit to have at least this 5 percent raise over four decades. (Note that the real GDP is the purchasing power of what the current value of output buys. It is obtained by estimating a price index known as GDP deflator. By contrast, per-capita GDP is real GDP divided by population.)

Wages had also been stagnant in most of the nations. According to a study by McKinsey Global Institute, up to 70 percent of people in

25 developed economies had seen no rise in their incomes between 2005 and 2014. The study focused specially on six nations including the United States, UK, France, the Netherlands, Italy, and Sweden. Ninety-seven percent of Italy's families saw flat or falling incomes during the recession decade ending in 2014 compared to 80 percent for the United States, 63 percent for France, and 70 percent for the UK and the Netherlands. Sweden did the best, where incomes declined for only 20 percent of the families.

2.6   Rising Poverty

The Great Recession has also raised poverty sharply in many countries. Even the United States, one of the richest in the world, has seen a big rise in poverty. According to the 2017 Economic Report of the President, about 14 percent of Americans lived below poverty line in 2015, which is around where it was in 1967 when President Lyndon Johnson started his war on poverty. In 2007, the poverty rate was 12.5 percent and reached a peak of 15 percent in 2012, which according to the Census Bureau was the worst in almost 50 years. It is clear that the welfare programs such as food stamps, cash grants to very poor families, medical care, and cheap housing have yet to make a dent in poverty. By some estimates, the United States has spent more than $20 trillion to fight the war on poverty. In 2014 alone, the nation spent almost $1 trillion for this war. It looks like this war will never be over and the government will have to provide increasing amounts of money to prevent poverty from rising further.

Recessions are bad for poverty and the Great Recession was worse. The Great Depression was the worst, but the question is this: Is rising government spending the right answer for the war on poverty? We will study this question in detail in Chapter 6, but for now it seems to be clear that some new approach is needed to reduce poverty.

Poverty has also risen sharply in many other countries since 2007. Jessica Hartogs, citing a report issued by the ILO in 2016, writes that poverty has increased recently in developed countries, especially Europe. This should not be surprising because recessions often do this, in spite of a vast network of welfare spending that exists in Europe.

Summary

This chapter tells us where the world stood in 2017, in terms of economic growth, unemployment, debt, wage stagnation, inequality, and poverty. The picture does not look bright even though almost the entire world had printed vast amounts of money and raised government budget deficits sharply since the start of the Great Recession.

Bibliography

Batra, Ravi. *Greenspan's Fraud: How Two Decades of His Policies Have Undermined the Global Economy.* Palgrave Macmillan, New York, 2005.

Batra, Ravi. *The New Golden Age: The Coming Revolution against Political Corruption and Economic Chaos.* Macmillan, 2009.

Bjonnes, Roar, Hargreaves, Caroline. *Growing a New Economy: Beyond Crisis Capitalism and Environmental Destruction.* Innerworld Publications, Puerto Rico, 2017.

Condon, Christopher, Boesler, Matthew. *Five Questions About the Fed's $4.5 Trillion Balance Sheet.* Bloomberg Markets, June 6, 2017. https://www .bloomberg.com/news/articles/2017-06-06/five-questions-about-the -fed-s-4-5-trillion-balance-sheet

Dobbs, Richard, Madgavkar, Anu, Manyika, James, Woetzel, Jonathan, Bughin, Jacques, Labaye, Eric, and Kashyap, Pranav. *Poorer than Their Parents? A New Perspective on Income Inequality, McKinsey Global Institute Report.* July 2016. http://www.mckinsey.com/global-themes/employment-and-growth/ poorer-than-their-parents-a-new-perspective-on-income-inequality

Economic Report of the President. U.S. Government Publishing Office, 2017. https://www.gpo.gov/fdsys/pkg/ERP-2017

Hartogs, Jessica. *Poverty Increasing in Developed Countries: ILO.* Special to CNBC. May 19, 2016. https://www.cnbc.com/2016/05/19/poverty-increasing-in-developed-countries-ilo.html

Keen, Steve. Don't Trust Ben Bernanke On Helicopter Money, April 12, 2016. https://www.forbes.com/sites/stevekeen/2016/04/12/dont-trust-ben-bernanke-on-helicopter-money/#938e3573e42f

Mulay, Apek. *Mass Capitalism: A Blueprint for Economic Revival.* Book Publishers Network, Bothell, 2014.

Mulay, Apek. *How the Information Revolution Remade the Business and the Economy: A Roadmap for Progress of the Semiconductor Industry.* Business Expert Press, LLC., New York, 2017.

CHAPTER 3

Macroeconomics of Income and Wealth Concentration

3.1 Introduction

In April 2014, the International Monetary Fund (IMF) organized a seminar on the economic effects of income and wealth inequality and declared: "Rising income inequality is, by now, universally acknowledged as a critical economic, social and political issue and one that is not confined to a particular group of countries or any particular region of the world." During the election year 2016, almost every politician agreed with IMF. Such a message came from Bernie Sanders to Hillary Clinton to Donald Trump, and several other potential presidential candidates. Liberals and many conservatives talked about how growing income and wealth disparities in the United States had destroyed the American dream for the poor and the middle class.

Until 2007, this type of talk was limited to liberal politicians and economists, and conservatives either denied that disparities existed or said that they were good for the economy in raising savings, investment, and economic growth that benefitted everyone in society. The start of the Great Recession brought about a major change in this type of thinking.

So long as people had jobs the public did not pay much attention to the economic effects of inequality. Even in 2008, when Barrack Obama won the election, it was health care not general inequality that was the major issue that brought him victory. The recession had started in December 2007 and by the time Obama took charge in January 2009, the recession had spread widely in the United States and around the world. Thousands of people were laid off every month and though the rich also suffered somewhat from the stock-market crash the general public was totally devastated.

The health-care reform was enacted in 2009, but it did not bring relief to the unemployed. The Federal Reserve began to print lots of money and the government sharply raised its budget deficit. The economy began to stabilize and then the National Bureau of Economic Research (NBER) declared the end of the recession. Once the recession was declared over the stock market began to behave as if everything was normal again. The rich began to get richer from rising share prices. CEOs started getting big pay raises along with stock options, while unemployment kept rising. That is when the public began to pay attention to the issue of income and wealth disparities.

As the Federal Reserve printed increasing amounts of money, both the federal funds rate and interest rates fell steadily. The retirees now began to suffer. They had relied on interest income from their savings, but Certificate of Deposit (CD) rates fell nearly to zero. CDs that had earned as much as 5 percent in 2007 earned just 1 percent by 2010. The unemployed were suffering already, but the Federal Reserve policies created suffering for the retirees also. The ones who benefitted from all this were the rich, as shown in Figures 3.1, 3.2, and 3.3. The government was content to make sure that the unemployed did not starve and extended their unemployment benefits again and again.

Until 2007, the unemployment benefits were available for 6 months, but with the recession going on and on, they were supplement by extended benefits. As unemployment persisted extended benefits themselves were extended again and again, and eventually lasted for up to 99 weeks. The extended benefits were terminated in 2013.

The lasting suffering of the elderly retirees and the unemployed, especially the long-term unemployed, along with the fact that the rich again were getting richer after 2009, began to raise the public awareness of the presence of rising inequality. The financial institutions of Wall Street, especially the big banks, brokerages, and insurance companies, generated a lot of irritation among the people because of their rising incomes. They had earned huge incomes prior to the recession and when some of them became bankrupt the government including the Federal Reserve had bailed them out. All this created great resentment among the people.

Percent

Figure 3.1 National income share accruing to top 1 percent of families: 1915–2012

Note: This graph draws on the work of Thomas Piketty and Emmanuel Saez.
Source: Council of Economic Advisers, *The Economic Report of the President*, 2014.

2012 dollars

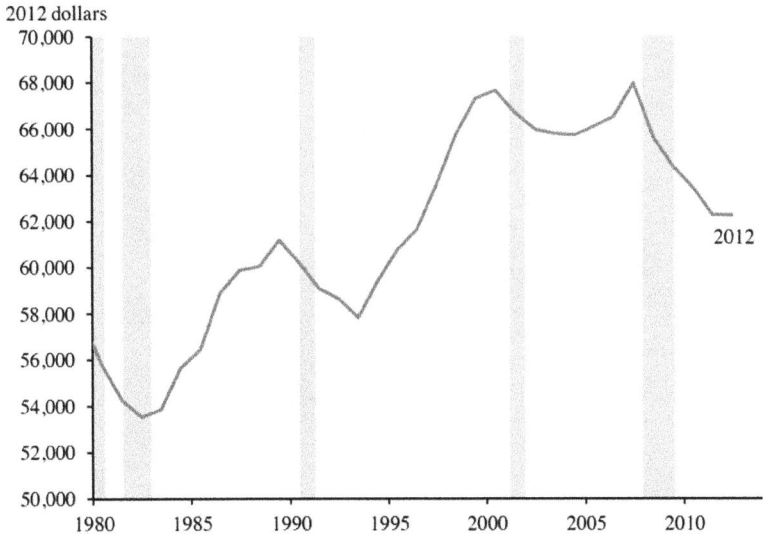

Figure 3.2 Real income for the median family: 1980–2012

Source: Council of Economic Advisers, *The Economic Report of the President*, 2014.

Finally, a movement called "Occupy Wall Street" began in Zuccotti Park of New York City in September 2011 which focused on how the government had first bailed out some of the financial institutions that were now getting richer with stock prices rising sharply even when the general public continued to suffer from the effect of the Great Recession. Few people even believed that recession was over.

The movement created new awareness among the people of the rising gap between the incomes of the top 1 percent of the families and the remaining 99 percent. People began to recognize that political corruption and corporate money power were interlinked. Within a few months, the Occupy Wall Street movement became a global movement. The phrase "99 percent versus 1 percent" entered the public consciousness. Economists also began to pay attention to the issue of inequality.

3.2   Inequality Economics in the 20th Century

The effects of income inequality had been analyzed before the start of the recession, but not extensively. Keynes had raised this question by saying that the rich have a lower marginal propensity to consume (mpc) than the poor so that as income inequality rises consumption spending goes down or savings go up. This tends to reduce demand relative to supply

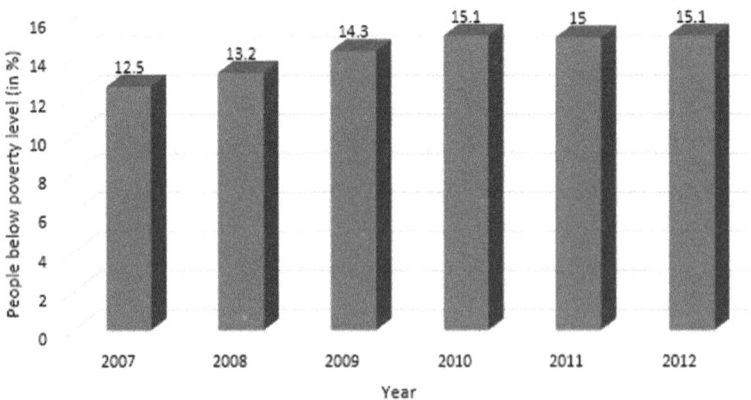

Figure 3.3 People below poverty level (2007–2012)

Source: Ravi Batra, End Unemployment Now, p. 22. Other Source: U.S. Census Bureau, 2014.
'People below poverty level' is the standard measure of the rate of poverty.

and thus start a recession. He had thus offered an argument in favor of reduced inequality and progressive income taxation. Others had used this argument for the redistribution of income through government policy.

Let us suppose the government lowers the tax burden of the poor by $100 and raises that of the rich by $100. If the mpc of the rich is 60 percent and of the poor is 90 percent, then the rich will cut their spending by $60 and the poor will raise their spending by $90, so that there will be a rise in overall spending of $30. This raises aggregate demand by $30, which raises the output by $30. This redistribution of income through taxation raises output and even employment.

Some economists challenged this argument by saying that savings fall by $30 from this redistribution. A fall in savings eventually causes a fall in investment, and since investment is needed for capital formation and new technology, this causes a fall in labor productivity and hurts economic growth. These economists offered a growth argument against redistribution policies. Such economists mostly favor neoclassical economics, which believes that inequality exists because of differentials in skills. They believe in the marginal productivity theory of distribution, which says that everyone earns in accordance with their productivity. Marginal product is the output of the last worker hired and since there is only one CEO, his output is his marginal product. So, if a CEO earns millions of dollars in salary and benefits, then he deserves them because they represent his marginal productivity. If the government taxes them heavily then his productivity and work incentive will fall and hurt the entire economy.

In 1987, Prof. Ravi Batra created a storm in the economics profession. He agreed with Keynes that rising income inequality may lead to a recession, but he argued that a depression results from a sharp rise in wealth concentration. He used historical data to show that wealth disparity rose sharply before every depression. For example, the top 1 percent of families owned 36 percent of wealth in 1929, which was the highest until then and that is why the depression was also the worst.

Batra argued that the stock market plays a crucial role in the start of a depression. A rise in wealth concentration leads to stock speculation as the wealthy are more prone to taking risks than the poor. For a multimillionaire or a billionaire, a small return on investment does not mean much. For someone earning a million dollars per year, a return of

3 percent bringing $10,000 on investment does not mean much. Such people want higher returns which are available only through speculation. So, as wealth concentration rises, speculation rises and over the years the stock market goes into a bubble. A time comes when the market crashes and starts a depression.

Batra started his analysis in 1983 in two articles and predicted a sharp increase in share prices resulting from rising wealth concentration, which he believed would crash by 1990. He put his arguments in a self-published book in 1985. As the Dow Jones Index broke records from 1983 to 1987, Batra's analysis and stock-market predictions gained credibility and a major publisher took over his publication. The stock market crashed in October 1987 and Batra's book became a best seller and remained on the best-selling list for 52 weeks. The forecast was not completely accurate because the market had crashed 2 years before 1990, but his argument that high wealth concentration creates depressions created a storm in the economic profession, which sharply denounced his argument.

Batra had also predicted a global depression in the 1990s, but only a recession occurred in 1990, although in Japan there was a depression. Since the depression did not spread to the United States, Batra lost credibility and his powerful argument against wealth concentration was ignored by economists.

So, in the 20th century, economists were divided into those who viewed inequality as bad and those who thought it was good. But the view is very different now. Most economists today think that inequality is good up to a point, but excessive inequality hurts the economy.

3.3   Inequality Economics in the New Millennium

Due to various reasons, income and wealth disparities started to rise after 1981 when supply-side economics became a government policy. Income tax rates fell for both individuals and corporations, whereas most other types of taxes, especially the social security and the self-employment tax, rose sharply. Since the social security tax is not progressive and is imposed only on a portion of a person's wage, it falls heavily on the poor and the middle class. So, inequality began to rise after 1981.

When Batra wrote his book in 1985, such tax policies had not fully shown their effects, and mainstream economists were not interested in this subject. By the end of the century, income and wealth disparity had begun to rise but mainstream economists still showed no interest in this subject. But, after the recession, when the effects of inequality could not be ignored, some notable economists such as Professors Joseph Stiglitz and Paul Krugman wrote about it. Both of them have won Nobel prizes.

Professor Stiglitz wrote an influential book in 2012, *The Price of Inequality*. Stiglitz argues that society pays a big price by ignoring the harmful effects of rising inequality, which results mainly from the wealthy controlling politicians and regulatory authorities. This control gives the rich enormous power to shape laws, especially tax laws, in their favor and against everyone else. He begins his book suggesting that high inequality weakens the system of justice. Those responsible for the Great Recession should have been punished but that did not happen. He writes:

> A basic sense of values should, for instance, have led to guilt feelings on the part of those who were engaged in predatory lending, who provided mortgages to poor people that were ticking time bombs, or who were designing the 'programs' that led to excessive charges for overdrafts in the billions of dollars. (p. xvii)

Some banks and financial institutions were fined, but they considered it merely the price of business. In some cases, the fine was enormous but no larger than 6 month's profits. The fine showed the enormity of their crimes, but the punishment was only a little monetary loss. The current system is one where justice can be bought.

Some economists argue that high inequality results from globalization and technological change. But Stiglitz disagrees with this view. He writes, "While there may be underlying forces at play, politics have shaped it in ways that advantage the top at the expense of the rest."

The conservative scholars usually believe that free markets are the solution for every economic problem. Stiglitz basically agrees with this view but argues that markets are no longer competitive when the 1 percenters control politics and the media through their money. The reduction in estate tax and the removal of controls on corporate contributions for political campaigns have made markets uncompetitive. They have increased corporate monopoly power and such power makes the marginal productivity theory invalid.

CEOs' incomes, according to Stiglitz, do not reflect high productivity but high market shares that enable very large companies to set high prices for their products and pay low wages. High inequality is aided by government policy. He writes:

American inequality didn't just happen. It was created. . . .

Much of the inequality that exists today is a result of government policy, both what the government does, and what it does not do. (p. 28)

The government, for instance, awards a big contract to just one company to supply some goods and the company charges huge prices for those goods. The company makes big profits not through competition but through the restriction of competition. Such policies are very frequent and lead to high profits.

In December 2016, President-Elect Trump pointed out that Boeing had been awarded a contract to build Air Force One, which is a special airplane used by presidents and their cabinet officers. He complained that Boeing's price of $4 billion for just one plane was excessive. This is an example of how some government suppliers make excessive profit from their government contracts. This is also an example of how government policy generates inequality in the economy.

Stiglitz thinks competition among firms is good, but the government regulations are necessary to keep the firms competitive because monopoly power awarded to a few firms is as bad as excessive regulation.

In a more recent essay, Stiglitz summarizes his argument presented in his book *The Price of Inequality*. He argues that it is not difficult to reduce inequality, as he writes:

We need more investment in public goods; better corporate governance, antitrust and anti-discrimination laws; a better regulated financial system; stronger workers' rights; and more progressive tax and transfer policies. By "rewriting the rules" governing the market econ-

omy in these ways, it is possible to achieve greater equality. . . . (https://
evonomics.com/joseph-stiglitz-inequality-unearned-income/)

3.4   Professor Krugman

Another well-read book on how inequality caused the recession came
from Professor Paul Krugman. The title of this book, written in 2012,
End This Depression Now, suggests that Krugman thinks that the crisis
of 2007 was not just a recession; it was a depression. In other words,
Krugman, like Keynes, wrote his book to end a depression; his arguments
are mostly the same as those offered by Keynes.

Keynes argued that spending and income are interrelated. If income
is high, spending is high, but if spending is high, production and hence
income are high. In his chapter 3, Krugman argues, "your spending is my
income, and my income is your spending." His argument is thus similar
to that of Keynes.

The Great Recession and the Great Depression had several events in
common. In both cases, there was a housing meltdown prior to a stock-market
crash; consumer debt went up sharply in the decade before the downturn;
the housing meltdown and the market crash led to a severe banking crisis,
and once a recession started, interest rates fell sharply. Similarly, income and
wealth inequality jumped prior to the start of the crisis.

As interest rates moved toward zero, the economy was caught in a
liquidity trap in which monetary policy becomes ineffective. Krugman,
like Keynes, argued that the only effective policy left then is fiscal expansion. He advised the Obama administration to raise the budget deficit
above what was already a huge amount. He said there was no need for
high unemployment to persist long after the recession was declared over
if only the government had the will to end the crisis by further increasing
spending.

Krugman cited the case of public works projects that FDR (President
Roosevelt) had created during the 1930s and argues that after 1936
employment rose and income inequality fell. He advised President
Obama to adopt the policies of FDR.

Another influential economist, Professor Jeffery Sachs, also dis-
likes the fact that income and wealth disparities have shown a steady

rise in recent years. In his latest book, published in 2017, he calls for increasing government spending for infrastructure rather than consumer demand:

> The nation's core infrastructure . . . is now at least a half-century old, and much of it is falling into disrepair . . . The chronic underinvestment in infrastructure dates back at least thirty years, essentially since the completion of the interstate highway system. (p. 28)

This is where he differs somewhat from neo-Keynesian economists such as Stiglitz and Krugman.

3.5   Inequality and Macroeconomic Performance

How does inequality affect macroeconomic performance? We will now show that macro policy becomes less effective in the presence of inequality because it reduces the positive effects of the Keynesian multiplier. According to the 2017 Economic Report of the President, federal debt rose by $3.5 trillion from 2000 to 2007, while GDP rose by $4.2 trillion.

As shown in Table 3.1, the debt multiplier was greater than one, because production rose faster than debt. In the meanwhile, inequality had continued to rise. In the next 7 years, debt rose by $9 trillion, but GDP rose by only $2.7 trillion. In the first case,

$$\text{Debt multiplier} = 4.2/3.5 = 1.2.$$

Table 3.1 Government debt and GDP 2000–2014

Year	Government debt (in trillion USD)	GDP (in trillions)
2000	5.6	10
2007	8.9	14.2
2014	17.9	17

Source: Council of Economic Advisers. The Economic Report of the President, 2017, Table B17, p. 584.

In the second case,

$$\text{Debt multiplier} = 2.8/9 = 0.3.$$

These figures must be very disturbing to Keynes because, according to his theory, the spending multiplier is greater than one, especially when a nation has a lot of unemployment as during 2007 to 2014. Fiscal policy had nearly zero effectiveness because the multiplier of 0.3 is not far from zero. The normal value of this is 3, but high inequality lowers its value sharply.

This analysis confirms Stiglitz's argument that high inequality lowers macroeconomic performance, but it does in a simple way. Many other studies have offered the same conclusion. How rising inequality reduces the effectiveness of Keynesian policies is examined in detail in Chapter 6.

3.6   Empirical Research

Some empirical studies appearing since 2007 also demonstrate that rising inequality hurts economic growth. This is the conclusion from several economists such as Dr. Tuomas Malinen who wrote a dissertation on this subject using data about Finland's economy. A 2014 study by OECD also supports this view. "This compelling evidence proves that addressing high and growing inequality is critical to promote strong and sustained growth and needs to be at the centre of the policy debate," said OECD Secretary-General Angel Gurría. "Countries that promote equal opportunity for all from an early age are those that will grow and prosper." (http://www.oecd.org/newsroom/inequality-hurts-economic-growth.htm)   Two other economists, Bebonchu Atems and Jason Jones, use a sophisticated econometric model to come to the same conclusion.

Summary

This chapter shows that following the recession of 2007 many studies have appeared to document the harmful effects of income and wealth disparities. No longer is this an ethical question because growing inequality hurts economic growth. Furthermore, I have shown that the macroeconomic policy also fails to have desired effects because the debt multiplier turned out to be close to zero after 2007.

Bibliography

Batra, Ravi. *The Great Depression of 1990*. Venus Books of Dallas, Texas,1985. (Republished by Simon & Schuster in 1987.)

Brueckner, Markus, Norris, Era Dabla, Gradstein, Mark. "National Income and Its Distribution", *Journal of Economic Growth* 20:149–175, 2015.

Galor, Oded. "Inequality, Human Capital Formation, and the Process of Development", Brown University working papers 2011-7.

Galor, Oded, Zeira, Joseph. "Income Distribution and Macroeconomics", *Review of Economic Studies*. 1993; 60:35–52.

IMF Policy Paper—*Fiscal Policy and Income Inequality*. January 23, 2014. https://www.imf.org/external/np/pp/eng/2014/012314.pdf

Krugman, Paul. *End This Depression Now!* W. W. Norton & Company, New York, 2012.

Malinen, Tuomas. Income Inequality in the Process of Economic Development: An Empirical Approach. December 2011. https://helda.helsinki.fi/bitstream/handle/10138/28517/incomein.pdf?sequence=1

Stiglitz, Joseph. *The Price of Inequality: How Today's Divided Society Endangers Our Future*. W. W. Norton & Company, New York, 2012.

Taylor, Alan. *Occupy Wall Street*. The Atlantic. https://www.theatlantic.com/photo/2011/09/occupy-wall-street/100159/

CHAPTER 4

The Environment and Macroeconomics

Environmental economics is a controversial subject because a good part of this literature believes in the phenomenon of global warming occurring through man-made climate change, and some experts including some scientists are not sure if this warming is a natural part of the weather cycle or is caused by human activity. But there is no doubt that the global environment has become very polluted and there is a lot of research that shows that much of this pollution has resulted from the burning of fossil fuels such as coal, petroleum, and gasoline. The world has rapidly industrialized to raise its economic growth and reduce poverty, but this growth means an increasing use of oil and gasoline, which in turn means polluted air especially in large cities like Los Angeles, New Delhi, Beijing, and many others.

Air is very polluted in most countries, so are rivers from the release of chemicals by many industries. Oceans are also polluted from excessive shipping that transports goods across countries. Global warming may be controversial but pollution is very real.

The pollution of the environment has been normally studied in the area of microeconomics, but recently macroeconomics has also paid attention to it. That is exactly what we study in this chapter.

4.1   GDP and GNH

The gross domestic product (GDP) has been used as a measure of economic activity and national well-being for a long time. But it is not considered the best measure; a better measure is said to be net domestic product (NDP), which is

$$NDP = GDP - \text{Capital depreciation}.$$

The idea is that the wear and tear of capital stock should be deducted from total production to get a better measure of economic activity. A new concept has become popular in recent years to measure gross national happiness (GNH), with GDP or material well-being only a part of what makes people happy, which is what everyone wants to be.

GNH is mostly a philosophical concept and is not easy to measure. It was discovered by Jigme Sigye Wangchuck, the King of Bhutan, which is situated in the northeastern part of India. The king emphasized that a nation's happiness depends not only on a good living standard but also on good government, environment, and sustainable economic development, so that a nation's natural resources are properly used for current and future generations. GNH has more recently attracted the attention of UN economists and environmentalists.

Thus, a good government, a pollution-free environment and a decent living standard are the three ingredients of people's happiness.

4.2   The Circular Flow

One idea introduced by Keynes is called the circular flow that prevails in a macro economy. The circular flow is that the revenue of firms comes mainly from consumer spending and the incomes of people come from that revenue. The model is presented in Figure 4.1. The firms expect or estimate a certain level of demand for goods and services produced by them and offer that much output to consumers, who buy this output at a certain price from money that they earn from working for the firms. Thus, money flows from consumers to firms, which then return it to the same consumers in the form of wages, rent, interest, and dividends. Firms offer goods and families offer them factors of production in the form of labor and capital.

This interdependence of markets underlies the income multiplier that we studied in Chapter 2. In the context of environmental economics, the circular flow also includes the biosphere and the use of natural resources, because production occurs not only from the use of labor and capital but also from the use of land, water, air, minerals, which are the natural resources, if these resources are depleted or polluted, then their

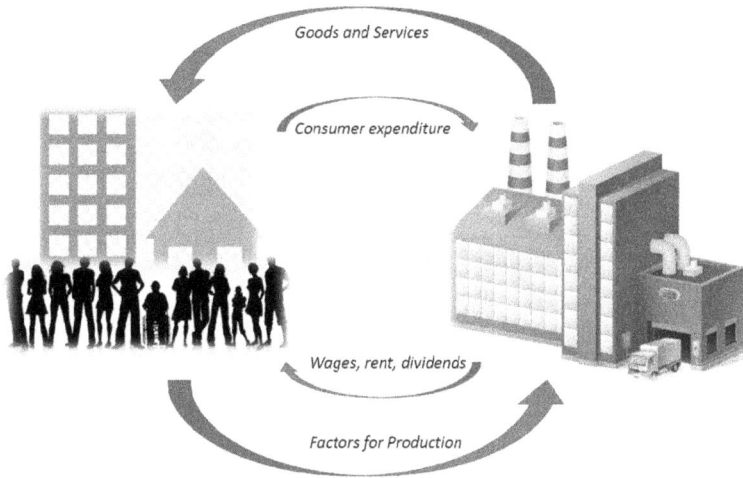

Figure 4.1 The standard circular flow model in Keynesian economics

Source: Harris, Jonathan M., Codur, Anne-Marre. *Macroeconomics and the Environment*, p. 1.

costs should be included in the estimates of GDP or national income. This is the main idea that the environment should be a part of any circular flow model.

There is natural capital and there is produced capital, and while the depletion of produced capital is part of NDP, we should also include the depletion of natural capital to estimate the true level of output available to society. Otherwise, NDP is an overestimate of an economy's output. The circular flow diagram that includes the biosphere is presented in the Figure 4.2.

The true concept of NDP is then

NDP = GDP – Capital Depreciation – Resource Depreciation.

Resource depreciation is hard to estimate but the World Resources Institute (WRI) has provided estimates for a few countries. WRI estimated depletions for 3 years of resources such as forestry, petroleum, and soil. In the case of Indonesia, for example, resource depreciation amounted to 9 percent of GDP per year. This is a very substantial amount and shows how important are the costs of pollution.

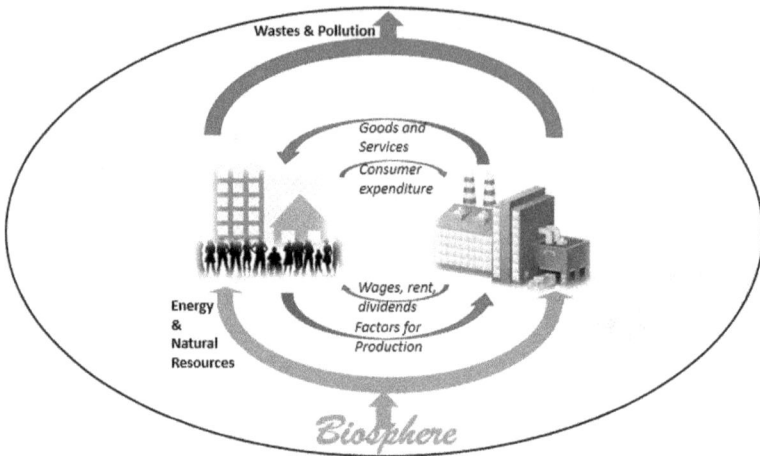

Figure 4.2 The circular flow linked to the biosphere

Source: Harris Jonathan and Codur Anne-Marre, *Macroeconomics and the Environment*, p. 3.

The World Bank has provided estimates of resource depletion in the form of reduction in savings. For instance, for Saudi Arabia, which depends primarily on the production of oil, the nation used so much of its resource that its savings rate has been substantially negative. Such costs are real.

4.3 Macroeconomic Policy

Many environmentalists emphasize that there are limits to economic growth, but their warnings have been mostly ignored especially since the start of the Great Recession. But nations can devise such economic policies that raise employment, create growth, and provide good jobs. Fossil fuels can be replaced over time by forms of energy that are friendly to the environment. Solar energy, wind power, and hydroelectric power are a vast unlimited resource and are mostly free from pollution. Two economists Roar Bjonnes and Caroline Hargreaves have written a book *Growing a New Economy*, which offers a variety of ways in which an economy can grow fast while reducing pollution at the same time.

They write:

Science has concluded that pollution causes individual as well as collective problems—various cancers, as well as polluted rivers and

oceans full of plastic waste. Sometimes the price is very costly . . .
On a cold day in January 2000 a dam burst in Romania. The dam
contained toxic waste—one hundred thousand cubic meters of
cyanide-laden water . . . Cyanide is extremely toxic. Even a small
doze can be deadly to humans and animals alike . . . The mining
disaster killed at least 80 percent of the fish in the region, the
water became unsafe to drink, and environmental disease was no
longer just an abstract medical term—it became a personal health
problem for many people. (p. 220)

Bjonnes and Hargreaves note that there are limits to growth because
of the limits to environmental degradation. Yet they offer ways in which
growth may continue while the environment shows improvement. Some
of the ways that have been already implemented are as follows:

1. Fossil fuel subsidies fell 44 percent in 2009. . .
2. Continuing its rapid ascent, installed global wind power capacity
   increased 24 percent . . . in 2010.
3. Solar photovoltaic generating capacity grew even faster.
4. Global biofuel production increased 17 percent in 2010 . . .
5. Organic farming methods were used on 37.2 million hectares worldwide in 2009 . . . a 150 percent increase since 2000. (pp. 233–4).

In short, Bjonnes and Hargreaves have produced a virtual encyclopedia of how to generate environmental-friendly economic growth.

4.4   Keynesian Policy

One way to fight a recession is Keynesian policy of increasing budget
deficit through a tax cut and a rise in government spending. Normally,
the spending rise is directed to keep consumer demand from a continued fall that results from falling production. This was clear during the
recent recession as unemployment benefits were repeatedly extended for
the unemployed. The tax cut was also designed to keep disposable income
from falling too much and thus prevent a big decline in consumer spending. But the Obama administration also directed some spending toward

investments that are friendly to the environment. They included spending to make federal building energy efficient, grants to states to do the same, research on renewable energy production, and public transit to reduce dependence on cars.

Similarly, tax incentives were granted to solar industries, while the public received big tax credit for installing solar roofs and buying energy-efficient appliances. In other words, fiscal policy showed an understanding that environment matters a lot to the economy.

Even monetary policy was somewhat friendly to the environment. Electric cars and hybrid cars that give great mileage for gasoline use are more expensive than other cars. As interest rates fell sharply, the more expensive cars become affordable.

4.5   Carbon Taxes

Another way in which fiscal policy can become friendly to the environment is to change the mix of taxes. Taxes imposed on fossil fuels that increase air pollution, through the rise of carbon dioxide, are known as carbon taxes. Such taxes are those imposed on coal, oil, gasoline, natural gas, and so on. If these taxes go up in a big way, they will cut the demand for fossil fuels and improve the environment. But then they may lower consumer spending because a part of these taxes will be passed on to the consumers. But if suppose some other tax is lowered at the same time to keep the tax revenue constant, then consumption demand in the economy may remain constant or even go up. For instance, if a strong rise in a carbon tax is matched by a slight fall in the sales tax so that the revenue is constant, consumer spending could even rise because the sales-tax revenue is rather large and sales tax cut would mean a lot to consumers. This way tax policy can stimulate consumer demand and cut pollution at the same time.

4.6   Sin Taxes

A sin tax is one that cuts the consumption of things considered harmful to public health. Excise taxes on cigarettes, alcohol, and so on, are examples of such taxes. A rise in such taxes along with a sales-tax cut has the same effect as a rise in carbon taxes along with a fall in the sales tax. A cigarette tax increase will reduce smoking, improve people's health, and also reduce air pollution. The point is that fiscal policy can be used to raise consumer spending and cut pollution at the same time.

Summary

This chapter deals with the increasing awareness that economists have shown for environmental-friendly macroeconomics since the start of the Great Recession. While the phenomenon of global warming due to climate change still does not command full consensus, there is no doubt that global pollution continues to increase and so do its costs, especially in terms of mounting health problems all over the world. It is not hard to imagine that if the environmental degradation keeps up its breath-taking pace, a time may come when people may choose a stable environment over continued growth. However, fiscal policy can be devised that may be consistent with continued growth along with pollution reduction.

References

Bjonnes, Roar, Hargreaves, Caroline. *Growing a New Economy: Beyond Crisis Capitalism and Environmental Destruction.* InnerWorld Publications, Puerto Rico, 2017.

Harris, Jonathan M., Codur, Anne-Marie. Macroeconomics and the Environment Global Development And Environment Institute, Tufts University Medford. http://ase.tufts.edu/gdae

Kelly, Annie. *Gross National Happiness in Bhutan: The Big Idea from a Tiny State That Could Change the World.* December 1, 2012. https://www.theguardian.com/world/2012/dec/01/bhutan-wealth-happiness-counts

Neuhauser, Alan. *Obama Budget a Gas for Environmental Advocates.* The president's proposed spending plan would put plenty of green behind his green initiatives. U.S. News. February 2, 2015. https://www.usnews.com/news/articles/2015/02/02/obama-budget-spends-big-on-climate-clean-energy

World Resources Institute. *World Resources 1996-97: A Guide to the Global Environment.* Oxford University Press, New York, 1996.

CHAPTER 5

Stock Market and Macroeconomics

Traditionally, macroeconomics has not paid much attention to the behavior of the stock market. An article from Professors Stanley Fischer and Robert Merton concludes that "macro analysis should give more attention to the stock market." After the Great Recession, more attention has indeed been paid to the stock market behavior. There are many reasons for this. One reason is that there was a stock market crash in 2008 and 2009. This was on top of a crash that occurred in 2000 and 2001, and that was on top of a crash that occurred in 1987. In comparison, during the 20th century there was only one major crash before World War II—the famous crash of 1929. The point is that with the rise of Keynesian economics, stock market crashes have become more frequent. There seems to be a connection between Keynesian economics and the stock market crashes and we will study this in detail in the next chapter.

Another reason is that in spite of these crashes many more families have invested in the stock market compared to 1920s. Therefore, stock prices play a larger role in the prosperity of the nation. Yet another reason is that central banks around the world become nervous when share prices fall and their policies are tied to stock market performance. Whenever, stock markets crash, bankers immediately cut the federal funds rate and the market interest rates fall immediately. This was done by Alan Greenspan when the market crashed in 1987, and again in 2000. Ben Bernanke did the same in the market crash of 2008 to 2009. The rest of the world also cut interest rates sharply. Therefore, central bank behavior has become predictable because it has been tied to share prices.

5.1   The Efficient Market Hypothesis

Professor Eugene Fama offered a well-known theory for stock market behavior. It is known as the efficient market hypothesis (EMH). According to this theory, stock markets are efficient and incorporate the entire relevant information about the economy. Therefore, it is futile to try to beat the market through frequent trading or market timing, as share prices are always at their fair market value. It is then not possible for people to buy stocks below the fair market price or sell them above the fair market price. Most money managers who manage other people's money frequently buy or sell shares on behalf of their clients in the belief that they can outperform the average market price, but according to EMH this is not possible in the long run, though in the short run, a few money managers may outperform the market by taking advantage of some bargains. This happens if money managers buy risky stocks, but there are chances of losing money in a big way.

Since most money managers charge a commission for their trading shares, they are not fond of the EMH idea. Well-known tycoons like Warren Buffet have produced larger returns than the market average and become multibillionaires in the process. Their success shows that buying undervalued companies and making them profitable is a better investment strategy than buying stocks that represent the market average. But Warren Buffet is an exception and very few money managers can match his performance. A study by Morningstar shows that less than half of the money managers outperformed the market average over time. In other words, buying an exchange-traded fund (ETF) like SPY that represents the Standard & Poor's index would have been a better investment strategy than handing over money to some expert manager. Thus, EMH idea has a large number of critics and supporters but a few money managers believe in it.

5.2   Stock Market and the Economy

Share prices are related to the profits of firms and these profits depend on the state of the economy. If the economy grows, firms make good profit and their stock prices rise. But the economy cannot grow if the firms do not grow. So, the fortunes of firms and the economy are interconnected. Then what comes first—the growth of the economy or the growth of the firms?

Since the economy is made of firms, the growth of firms must create the growth of the economy. In order to grow, the firms have to invest more money in their companies. They may do so from their profits or from borrowed money. But the increase in investment occurs only if the firms are already making a good profit. Thus, profitable firms create not only a good economy but also high stock prices. This argument shows that when stock prices are high, the economy grows at a faster pace.

5.3   The Wealth Effect

The stock market affects the people and the economy in many ways. One of them is known as the wealth effect, which refers to the effect of a change in the value of one's wealth on spending. As stock prices rise, people feel richer even if they do not sell their shares. So, income does not rise from capital gains, but the wealth seems to rise from paper profits, which makes them spend more on goods and services. As consumer spending rises, output goes up and more jobs are created. This argument became very popular after 2009, when stock prices began to rise even when unemployment kept rising, as central bankers around the world thought that the printing of money would bring down interest rates, which makes stocks more attractive relative to other assets like bonds and savings accounts. The heads of European Central Bank and the Federal Reserve argued that the stock market optimism will create general optimism and will make people spend more. This would then raise output and employment.

This was also why Alan Greenspan had lowered interest rates sharply after the worst stock market crash in 1987, because a stock market crash has far worse wealth effect than a stock market rise. When stock prices rise, people start to buy luxury goods and borrow money to buy them. But if the stock market crashes, the paper profits go away and the debt stays. High debt along with the disappearance of paper profits make people very pessimistic, which results in consumer spending falling sharply. This is what happened in 1929 and led to the Great Depression.

However, such arguments have their critics, who argue that since stock market gains go mostly to the rich, who have a low marginal propensity to consume, the wealth effect of rising stock prices has an insignificant effect on consumer spending. They argue that rising home prices that make people feel more optimistic have larger effects on consumer spending. Such is an argument given by Dean Baker, author of *The End of Loser Liberalism*, at Center for Economic and Policy Research.

5.4   The Investment Effect

High stock prices also raise business investment, especially in an economy with rising optimism, because many firms make profits by selling stocks and in turn have more money to invest more. This is also the positive effect of rising stock prices. But the effect may be reversed, as in 1929, if the stock market falls sharply.

5.5   Pension Funds

There are many companies that manage the pension accounts of their clients and expect high returns for these. One of the reasons why a larger population is involved in stock markets now is because either they or their funds have sold bonds and bought shares, as bonds now offer very low interest rates. Stock owners believe that the government will support the stock market in case of a big fall. They have witnessed similar situations in 1987, 2001, and ever since 2009.

5.6   Anticipation Effects

While the current state of the economy has a strong effect on the stock market, the economic future sometimes may have an even stronger effect. On one hand, the stock market begins to fall if the economy slows down or a recession is expected. On the other hand, if the future looks better, the stock market starts to rise even before the recession is over. When the government starts printing money and increases its deficits, production rises gradually, but the stock market rises in anticipation of increasing production and employment.

5.7   The Rate of Interest

The rate of interest has a very strong effect on the stock market for many reasons. First, there is an inverse relationship between rates of interest and bond prices. At low interest rates, bond prices are high, due to which bonds become less attractive compared to stocks. Second, low interest rates tend to increase consumer spending and business investment, so the economy becomes stronger which in turn raises the stock market.

5.8   Modern Portfolio Theory

Another theory that offers investment advice to people is known as the modern portfolio theory or MPT. According to MPT, an investor should diversify his or her portfolio of stocks to minimize the risk associated with the stock market investment. In the long run, stocks offer a much higher return than many other investments like corporate and government bonds, and for this reason, people like to have a part of their money invested in a variety of stocks. But occasionally, a company may fail and declare bankruptcy, and if a person has invested all the money in that company that person may lose all his savings. For this reason, the MPT suggests to buy a variety of stocks so that if one company fails or does not live up to expectations, others may perform better than the failing company. In this way, an investor's overall stock portfolio could still show strong results.

The diversification should be done not only among various stocks but also among various assets. Thus, an investor may put some money in stocks, some money in bonds, and some money in other assets, such as gold or real estate. In general, bonds are less risky than stocks and offer a fixed return, whereas stocks offer dividends that are usually below the return on bonds. But stocks offer a possibility of appreciation over time; although bonds can also appreciate when the interest rates fall, that appreciation is limited. So, in the long run, the stock returns have been higher than bond returns. According to MPT, an investor should diversify among stocks and buy some bonds and perhaps other forms of assets too.

5.9   The Random Walk Theory

Another theory offering investment advice is the random walk hypothesis that was proposed by economist Professor Burton Malkiel. This theory argues that stocks behave randomly and the previous performance of any stock is no guarantee about its future performance. If a stock has done well in the past, it does not mean it will do well in the future. Stock prices are random and follow an unpredictable path.

Like the EMH, the random walk theory also believes that stock markets are efficient and incorporate the entire available information in the prices of different stocks. Therefore, it is not possible to do better than the stock market average price through active-portfolio management or market timing. Risky behavior may lead to higher returns but it can also produce big losses.

In an article in the *Wall Street Journal* in 2017, "Index Funds Sill Beat Active-Portfolio Management," Professor Malkiel presented evidence in support of this theory. He wrote that, "During 2016, two-thirds of active managers of large capitalization U.S. stocks underperformed the S&P 500 large-capital index." He added, "More than 90 percent of the active managers underperformed their benchmark indexes over a 15-year period." Thus, the random walk theory advises the investor to put money in a diversified index fund and not in actively managed funds.

5.10   Adaptive Markets

Stock market theories can be divided into two categories. Some people believe investors and stock markets are rational and efficient, whereas others believe that stock markets and investors are irrational and emotional. When stock prices rise for some time, people start to believe in EMH; when they crash or fall sharply, the irrational and emotional theory becomes popular. In a 2017 book, *Financial Evolution at the Speed of Thought*, Professor Andrew Lo argues that both views are correct. During good times when investors make money year after year, everyone likes the stock market and believes in the rationality principle, but during bad times when people lose a lot of money in the stock market they regret and consider their behavior irrational.

Professor Lo writes:

> From the mid-1930s to mid-2000s, a period of relatively stable financial markets and regulations, the assumptions (of the efficient market hypothesis) offered reasonable approximation of U.S. financial markets.

But

the Adaptive Markets Hypothesis, however, tells us that long periods of market efficiency and stability are not guaranteed: They depend on the stability of the overall environment. When there are big changes that have significant impact on that environment-including political, economic, social, or cultural shifts-markets are going to reflect those changes. (p. 254)

Almost everyone agrees that a major change has occurred in the economic and financial environment since 2007 when the Great Recession started. The Federal Reserve and other central banks believe that stock markets are indicators of a strong economy. Whenever stocks decline continuously even for a short period, banks become nervous and hold press conferences to assure investors that they would continue to print money. They call their policies Quantitative Easing (QE) and so far, there have been three rounds of QE—QE1, QE2, and QE3. These rounds brought the federal funds rate to nearly zero and kept them constant till 2015. The Federal Reserve raised the rate to 1.25 percent by 2017, which was still very low. This kept the QE going. In Europe and Japan, interest rates even turned negative and remained so even in 2017.

Investors adapted themselves to this new environment where the central banks would move to support share prices whenever there was even a short period of stock decline. Since bonds had already become expensive because of very low interest rates, stock prices broke many records. This is an example of adaptive markets. The investors came to believe in the theory, follow the Fed, or don't fight the Fed. According to a financial writer, John M. Mason, "During the economic recovery from the Great Recession, the Federal Reserve has been very vocal in its support of the stock market and its desire to see stock prices increase."

Summary

This chapter deals with the inter-relationship between a nation's stock markets and its economy. The two depend on each other. When the firms are profitable, output rises and the economy grows at a fast pace. Similarly, when the economy grows fast, firms become more profitable.

There are many theories of how stock markets behave over time. The efficient market theory says that stocks are always priced at a fair market value, so that a passive investment strategy is good for investors, and nothing is gained from frequent buying and selling of stocks. This is also the belief of the random walk theory. But there are those who believe in market timing and active management of their portfolios. Finally, according to the adaptive market hypothesis, stock markets are rational and efficient most of the time, but when markets begin to fall, investors become emotional and cautious. They then adapt to the new environment.

Bibliography

Amadeo, Kimberly. *The Great Depression: What Happened, What Caused It, How Did It End?* The Balance. August 11, 2017. https://www.thebalance.com /the-great-depression-of-1929-3306033

Dean, Baker. *The End of Loser Liberalism*, Center for Economic and Policy Research, 2011, p. 18.

Lo, Andrew W., *Adaptive Markets: Financial Evolution at the Speed of Thought.* Princeton University Press, New Jersey, 2017.

Malkiel, Burton G. *A Random Walk Down Wall Street - The Get Rich Slowly but Surely Book.* https://pdfs.semanticscholar.org/5a26/4c944640613fdc887d72 e3c3da0445e3e37c.pdf

Malkiel, Burton G. *Index Funds Still Beat 'Active' Portfolio Management. There Is No Better Way for Individuals to Invest in the Stock Market and Save for Retirement.* The Wall Street Journal June 5, 2017. https://www.wsj.com/articles /index-funds-still-beat-active-portfolio-management-1496701157

Mason, John M. *Stock Market Performance: Index Funds And Federal Reserve Policy.* Seeking Alpha, June 7, 2017. https://seekingalpha.com/article/4079542-stock-market-performance-index-funds-federal-reserve-policy

Mauldin, John. *Modern Portfolio Theory 2.0: The Best Investment Strategy Today.* Forbes, June 1, 2017. https://www.forbes.com/sites/johnmauldin/2017/06/01/modern-portfolio-theory-2-0-the-best-investment-strategy-today/#43892be41f8f

Ro, Sam. *Nobel Prize Winner Eugene Fama Explains Why You Have No Chance Of Beating The Market.* Business Insider, October 14, 2013. http://www .businessinsider.com/2013-nobel-prize-in-economics-2013-10

CHAPTER 6

The Wage-Productivity Gap

A Unified Theory of Macroeconomics

6.1   Introduction

The previous five chapters analyzed some conventional and new macro-economic theories. The conventional theories have been around for a few centuries, but many new theories have come up since 2007, when the Great Recession led economists and financial writers to question their old models that had failed to see the recession and its severity. There is now a great focus on the effects of income and wealth inequality on macro-economic performance; some economists look at the effects of environ-mental pollution on macroeconomic policy, and some others have paid attention to the role of the stock market in macro policy, especially mon-etary policy.

Readers may have noticed that there are numerous theories about macroeconomic questions, and all seemed to be valid for a while, but were given up when the reality turned out to be different. For a long time, classical and neoclassical models dominated economic policy, but they failed to predict the Great Depression, and were given up after the 1930s. Keynesian economics became popular after the depression but led people to believe that a similar depression could not happen again because the policy makers would use Keynesian measures to prevent it. But the Great Recession has changed that view and the world is still not free completely from its bad effects after more than a decade of using extreme Keynesian policies.

Most people think that no one foresaw the Great Recession coming. For example, Professor Krugman writes: "Few economists saw our current crisis coming, but this predictive failure was the least of the field's problems. More important was the profession's blindness to the very possibility of catastrophic failures in a market economy." But there is one person who foresaw it clearly and even warned about it in a number of books. He is SMU professor and my mentor, Professor Ravi Batra. He wrote a book *The New Golden Age* in 2006, one year before the recession started. Let us look at some of his published forecasts:

> The economy will steadily get worse with home prices falling and layoffs rising . . .

> The housing bubble appears to be a major event, which once had a lot of momentum but is now beginning to recede. Its starting point was 2001, when the interest rate started a panicky fall. It is likely to burst in 2008, give or take a year. The burst could start in 2007 and continue till 2009 . . .

> The economy could still face a steep recession but avoid the calamity of a depression. Unemployment could rise to the level of 10 percent or more. (pp. 173, 175, 179)

This seems to be an amazing forecast, as if someone had a crystal ball to gaze into the future. We now know that the housing market began to collapse in the middle of 2007, and the NBER said that the recession started in December 2007 and ended in June 2009. Both 2007 and 2009 appear in Professor Batra's forecast. According to the 2017 *Economic Report of the President*, the unemployment rate peaked at 10.5 percent in 2010. The figure "10 percent" also appears in this forecast.

Professor Batra also wrote about the future of oil prices:

> The oil bubble started in 2003 . . . The current bubble could go on until 2011 and then crash in 2012. (p. 175)

This forecast is slightly off because the oil price stayed above $100 per barrel until 2013 and then collapsed to its 2015 level of around $30 per barrel. In 2017, it averaged around $45.

Professor Batra based his forecasts on a new macroeconomic theory that he called the theory of the wage-productivity gap. I described some parts of this theory in my 2014 book *Mass Capitalism: A Blueprint for Economic Revival* and later authored two more books in 2015 and 2016 addressing the problems faced by the technological sector of the U.S. economy and offered practical solutions to solve these problems, using the wage-gap theory. Here, I analyze it in full detail, because it appears to offer answers to all the questions that have been raised since 2007 and had not been answered before. It is truly a revolutionary theory. In his 2012 book *Economics and Nature*, economist Navin Doshi calls it the unified theory of macroeconomics, much like the unified theory of physics. Doshi, like myself, has an engineering degree and frequently writes on current economic problems in a variety of blogs. In Doshi's words: "Here are some of the events that beg for analysis and understanding."

1. "Why are governments around the world, including USA, sinking in a sea of debt?"
2. "Why are American families drowning in debt?"
3. "Why did profits surge all over the world in the 2000s, then crashed and then surge again in 2009 and 2010 even as 20 million people remained jobless in the US?"
4. "Why are there frequent stock market bubbles and crashes in recent years?"
5. "Why do trade deficits and surpluses persist in the globe?"
6. "What are the real causes of unemployment, recessions and depressions?"

Is there any theory that can singly analyze all the questions raised above? Fortunately, there is one thesis that rises to this challenge, and that is the theory of the wage gap offered by Professor Batra. (p. 87).

Economics and Nature, written by Doshi in 2012, is a remarkable book itself. It is well written and deals with economic thought since the ancient times, starting as early as 300 BC. Very few books have done that. Doshi concludes: "It is indeed remarkable that what numerous economic schools fail to elucidate is explained by one idea, which may be properly called the unified theory of economics. The unified theory offered by Batra is similar to the grand idea of the unified theory of physics in science." (p. 88)

A question not appearing in Doshi's list is this: "Why is there so much income inequality and wealth concentration all over the world?" The wage-gap theory also answers this question.

6.2   The Wage-Gap Theory

Professor Batra first wrote about this theory in his 1999 book, *The Crash of the Millennium*, in which he predicted a stock-market crash in 2000 and 2001. This crash also happened in the years he predicted. Later he explained it in detail in a 2004 book, *Common Sense Macroeconomics*, which was revised in 2012. The best version of this theory appeared in his most recent book, *End Unemployment Now: How to Eliminate Joblessness, Debt and Poverty Despite Congress*, which he wrote in 2015. Here I use his models presented in 2004 and 2015.

Batra begins with a simple or balanced economy, where there is no budget deficit or foreign trade deficit. In equilibrium,

$$\text{Supply} = \text{Demand.}$$

Here macro supply equals real GDP (Y) and

$$Y = AL,$$

where A is the average product of labor and L is labor's employment. This equation is true by definition, because by definition

$$A = Y/L,$$

so that productivity (A) is output divided by employment, or output per person. Assuming that all consumption comes only from labor income and savings come from profits,

$$C = wL,$$

where C is consumer spending, and w is the real wage. Here wL is the nation's labor income. This is only a simplifying assumption, but it applies to the U.S. economy, where the rate of savings is extremely low and workers do not have much ability to save. Savings in the economy come mostly from the rich, who earn a lot from their capital investments that bring them profits. Initially, suppose the government sector is very small, there is no budget deficit, and no debt of any type, aggregate demand (AD) can be written as

$$AD = C + I,$$

where I is the investment.

Here, AD is macro demand in the absence of any debt.

In equilibrium,

$$Y = AL = AD.$$

Let WG be the wage-productivity gap. Then

$$WG = A/w.$$

There is also an equation for profits but that will be added later when the analysis examines questions about the stock market. According to Batra, the wage gap is at the center of all macroeconomic phenomena. If the wage gap is low and stable, the economy remains prosperous with no unemployment and little inflation. But if the wage gap rises and stays high, all sorts of problems occur in almost all sectors of the economy. In *Common Sense Macroeconomics*, Batra writes that a rising wage gap creates troubles:

> Why? Because wages are the main source of demand, productivity the main source of supply, and if the two are not in sync with each other, aggregate demand and aggregate supply cannot be in equilibrium for long . . . Whenever any country or region suffered a deep depression, or long term stagnation, you will find the presence of a persistent wage-productivity gap in the background. (p. 202)

There are also equations that Batra uses to explain his theory of the wage gap with the help of numerical examples. Suppose, for the time being, that prices are constant and

$$w = \$6, L = 100, A = \$8, \text{ and } I = \$200,$$

then the real wage is $6, employment is for 100 workers, investment (I) equals $200, and on average a worker produces $8 worth of output. Then

$$Y = AL = 8 \times 100 = \$800$$
$$C = wL = 6 \times 100 = \$600$$

and

$$AD = C + I = 600 + 200 = \$800.$$

In this example, both AD and AS equal $800, so that market for goods and services is in equilibrium. There is no recession, and no layoffs. But there may not be full employment if labor supply exceeds 100. If labor supply is 110 and 10 people have no job, the unemployment rate is about 9 percent. According to classical and neoclassical economics, if the real wage falls in this situation, unemployment disappears because labor demand goes up when the price of labor falls.

Suppose wage rate falls to $5, but productivity remains constant, so that the wage gap rises from 8/6 to 8/5. Now

$$Y = \$800$$
$$C = 5 \times 100 = \$500$$

and

$$AD = 500 + 200 = \$700$$

It is clear that supply now exceeds demand and there is overproduction. Some workers will now be laid off and unemployment will rise. According to Batra,

So you see the classical theory is totally bogus. Instead of solving the problem, this approach makes it worse. In fact, investment will also fall because of a decrease in consumer spending, and more layoffs will follow. (*End Unemployment Now*, p. 47)

The wage gap also rises if productivity rises but the wage rate remains constant. Suppose productivity value rises to $9 so that a worker produces $9 worth of output. Here again the wage gap rises. Now

$$Y = 9 \times 100 = \$900 \text{ and } AD = \$800.$$

Again, there is overproduction that leads to layoffs. In other words, whenever the wage gap rises, there is overproduction and layoffs follow. It should be clear now that the main cause of unemployment in a market economy is a rise in the wage gap. The cause of the rise in the wage gap will be discussed later.

The assumption of a constant price is not necessary. If the wage gap rises, prices are likely to fall, or inflation might turn into disinflation. In this case, things may get worse because the revenue of employers could fall even more. This is the main reason why central banks have expanded money supply around the world since 2007. They have been constantly worried about maintaining a 2 percent inflation rate because a price fall or disinflation can turn a minor recession into a big one.

A few studies have appeared since 2007 that support the wage-gap theory. I have already referred to the books by Doshi and two economists, Roar Bjonnes and Caroline Hargreaves. In 2017, Thorsteinn Thorgeirsson, Adviser to the Central Bank Governor of Iceland, wrote an article that concluded that the wage gap went up sharply in Iceland before the start of the Great Recession. Iceland was one of the worst-hit nations but has recovered nicely since 2014 as the wage gap fell.

6.3   Wage Gap and the Budget Deficit

Figure 6.1 shows the behavior of productivity and real wages between 1947 and 2013, and it shows the wage gap has been rising sharply since 1980. But the Great Recession did not occur until 2007. What happened

Index, 1947=100 (log scale)

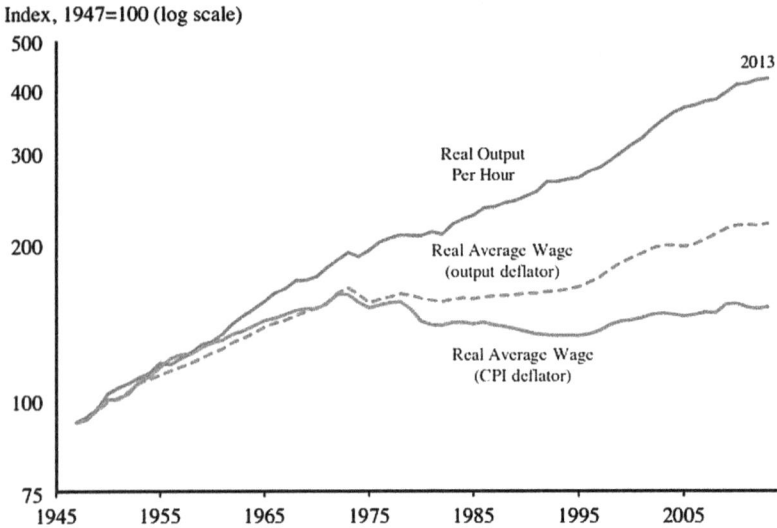

Figure 6.1 *Growth in productivity and average wage (1947–2013)*

Source: Council of Economic Advisers, *The Economic Report of the President*, 2014.

to wage-gap theory? The answer lies in the self-interest of the career politicians. In the United States, politicians face elections every 2 years or 4 years. At that time, they are afraid of facing the voters because when unemployment is high, many politicians lose their jobs. Angry voters make politicians nervous. The government then follows Keynesian policies in the interest of the unemployed workers.

Politicians or their economic advisers know that layoffs occur because demand is less than supply, and spending must rise to raise employment. The natural way is to follow policies that raise the real wage in proportion to the rise in labor productivity so that demand rises to the level of supply. For example, the government could raise the minimum wage in proportion to the rise in the Consumer Price Index (CPI) and productivity but that has not happened since 1980. The purchasing power of the federal minimum wage was down by more than 30 percent in 2017 compared to its level in 1969.

In addition to happy voters, a career politician also needs money for his election or re-election. He gets this money mostly from the rich people or rich corporations, who do not like to see a rise in the minimum wage. So, he does not want to create angry donors who could deny him the money. The only choice left to the politician is to raise the budget deficit either by raising government spending, or by cutting tax rates, or doing both.

When the Democratic Party is in charge of the government, the budget deficit rises mainly from increased government spending, and when the Republican Party is in charge the deficit rises mainly through a cut in the income tax rate. So, the budget deficit goes up whenever a recession occurs or when unemployment goes up. Since unemployment rises because of a rise in the wage gap, the rising wage gap creates the need for the rise in this deficit.

The needed rise in the deficit can be calculated from the numerical example. For example, in the case of the rise in productivity to $9,

$$Y = \$900.$$

But,

$$AD = \$800$$

So that

$$\text{Over production} = \text{Unsold goods} = 900 - 800 = \$100$$

This means that the budget deficit (BD) should rise by $100 to close the gap between supply and total spending. This policy is called fiscal expansion, and the government must now borrow this money to finance its new deficit. As a result,

$$\text{Total spending} = C + I + BD = AD + BD$$

In addition to fiscal expansion, the government acts through its branch of the Federal Reserve because government spending is much smaller than consumer and investment spending. The budget deficit is not enough to raise total spending to the level of supply. So, the Federal Reserve cuts interest rates to persuade consumers to borrow money and spend it, and calls it the policy of monetary expansion or quantitative easing. In this case,

$$\text{Total borrowing} = BD + CB$$

and

$$\text{Total spending} = AD + BD + CB,$$

where CB stands for consumer borrowing. For example, if the BD is $30, then CB must be $70 because to eliminate unsold goods

$$\text{Overproduction} = BD + CB$$

All this borrowing adds to the debt so that

$$BD + CB = \text{New debt}$$

and in equilibrium

$$AS = \text{Total spending} = AD + \text{New debt}$$

This is Professor Batra's fundamental equation of macro equilibrium, as shown in Figure 6.2, that explains why there is so much debt in America today. In other words, macro equilibrium nowadays does not mean that

$$\text{Supply} = \text{Demand}$$

It means that

$$\text{Supply} = \text{Demand} + \text{New debt},$$

where demand is money spent by consumers and investors from their incomes, and is different from total spending that includes total borrowing. I interviewed Professor Batra about his fundamental equation and asked him how debt could be a part of the equilibrium condition. He said,

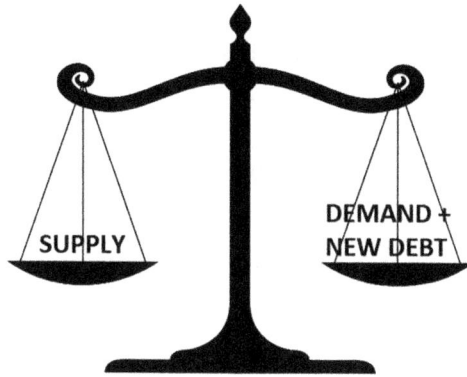

Figure 6.2 Modern representation of a balanced economy

Source: Batra, Ravi. *Commonsense Macroeconomics*, Cover Page, 2012.

New debt has become a part of equilibrium because the government now acts automatically to raise total spending whenever the spending falls short of the supply of goods and services. The government action is as predictable as that of markets, and so it is now a part of equilibrium. This is what explains why there is enormous debt at all levels in the United States. Consumers, students, federal, state and local governments are all drowning in an ocean of debt. But the main culprit is the rising wage gap along with the desire of most politicians to obtain campaign donations from the ultra-rich 1 percenters.

Batra's equilibrium equation indeed explains why debt has risen sharply since 1980 and continues to rise. If productivity rises every year and wages remain stagnant, then

$$Supply > Demand$$

every year. So, debt must rise every year to create equilibrium. Since productivity rises exponentially, then debt must rise exponentially. According to 2017 *Economic Report of the President*, productivity more than doubled between 1980 and 2016 while the real wage remained more or less constant. Since wage income is the main source of demand, supply rose much faster than demand and to raise spending to the level of supply, government debt rose every year, and as the Federal Reserve cut interest rates once in a while, consumers also borrowed money again and again. So, by 2017, both government debt and consumer debt, including student debt, broke new records.

The debt was huge even in 2012 when Doshi wrote his book and claimed that the wage-gap theory explains "Why are governments around the world, including USA, sinking in a sea of debt?" The wage gap has risen further since 2012 and so has government debt all over the world.

6.4   Wage Gap and Profits

The third question on Doshi's list is: "Why did profits surge all over the world in the 2000s, then crashed and then surged again in 2009 and 2010 even as 20 million people remained jobless in the US?" Actually, profits have risen even faster since 2010, while the economy has continued to stagnate. I raised this question in my interview with Professor Batra and his answer to this question simply shocked me. He said, "The federal government as well as the Federal Reserve are making the rich richer than ever before, because when wage gap and debt rise profits sky-rocket. The numerical examples in my books and the data demonstrate this decisively." He pointed to a graph on page 52 of his latest book, *End Unemployment Now*. This graph, reproduced as Figure 6.3 here, uses data compiled by *New York Times* and shows that the rate of profit under the Obama administration was near its all-time high, when the federal debt almost doubled.

Figure 6.4 conveys a similar idea. This one looks at the rate of profit rather than the share of profit from 1947 to 2011. The wage-gap theory says that there are two main influences on the rate of profit. One is the wage gap and the other is the level of government spending and debt. The 1940s were a war decade during which the government spending and debt went up sharply. The profit rate was also high and it is represented by the 1947 figure of 16 percent. The war had just ended and then the government spending and debt began to fall. By 1950, the profit rate fell to about 14 percent. The wage gap during the 1940s was stable, as the real wage kept pace with productivity (see Figure 6.1). From 1950 to 1970, the wage gap either fell or remained stable, while the war debt was

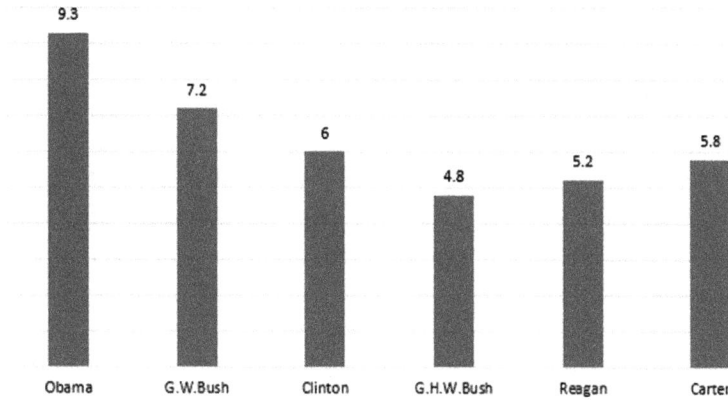

Figure 6.3 *After-tax corporate profits as share of GDP under various presidents (in %)*

Source: Batra, Ravi. *End Unemployment Now*, p. 52. Other Source: *The New York Times*, April 4, 2014.

retired. The profit rate also fell steadily. By 1970, it had fallen to a low of 8 percent, which is half of what it was in 1947. Clearly, as the wage gap fell or stabilized, and as the government debt fell, the profit rate also

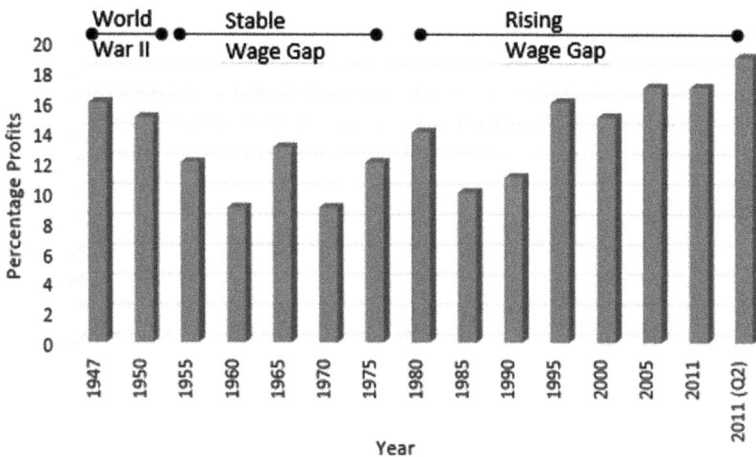

Figure 6.4 *Rate of profit in selected years (in %): 1947–2011*

Source: Batra, Ravi. *End Unemployment Now*, p. 53 . Other Source: Council of Economic Advisors, *The Economic Report of the President*, 1975 and 2013.

fell, and further fell sharply. From 1980 onward, the wage gap and the government debt began a steady rise. The profit rate hit an all-time high of 19 percent. Clearly, the rising wage gap along with government debt make the rich richer.

Professor Batra uses an equation for profits to prove his theory. Economists usually think that capital and labor are the main factors of production so that all production is divided between labor income and profits, which represent income to the owners of capital. In equilibrium,

$$\text{GDP} = Y = \text{Labor Income} + \text{Profits}$$

or

$$\text{Profits} = Y - \text{Labor income}.$$

But in disequilibrium when there is overproduction

$$\text{Profits} = Y - \text{Labor income} - \text{Unsold goods}$$

This is because the profit of any firm falls by the value of unsold goods. Going back to the numerical example, initial values are

$$w = \$6, L = 100, A = \$8, \text{ and } I = \$200.$$

With the economy in equilibrium initially, unsold goods = 0 and $Y = AD = \$800$, and with

$$C = wL = \$600,$$
$$\text{Profits} = 800 - 600 = \$200.$$

If productivity rises to $9, and the wage rate is constant, then as explained before, there are unsold goods of $100, so that

$$\text{Profits} = 900 - 600 - 100 = \$200$$

In spite of a rise in productivity, profits do not change because of the presence of unsold goods. But this is the predebt profit income when the economy is in disequilibrium. When monetary and fiscal expansion create new debt of $100 to generate equilibrium with zero unsold goods, then

$$\text{Profits} = 900 - 600 = \$300.$$

Before the debt, the profit is still $200, but in the post-debt equilibrium, when the companies are able to sell their entire production, profits rise to $300. What is more interesting is that profits rise by the full amount of the new debt.

If production goes up and the real wage falls, which happened during the 1980s and from 2007 to 2009, then the wage gap increases sharply, and profits may actually fall because of a big rise in unsold goods, but as soon as the government creates new debt, then profits start to rise and rise enormously. In this case, Prof. Batra writes:

> If wL or labor income falls, profits may or may not rise, and may actually decline, because unsold goods then certainly go up. If the government follows a policy of debt creation to absorb unsold goods, then it is clear that profits will rise close to the level of new debt, because then unsold goods fall to zero, unemployment vanishes and wL may stay constant. All this explains why the rate and share of profits neared their all-time high in 2014. (*End Unemployment Now*, p. 224)

6.5   Inequality and Wealth Concentration

A chapter in the 2017 *Economic Report of the President* deals with the question of income inequality and wealth concentration in the United States. It starts with the following quote:

> In 2013, President Obama declared inequality "the defining challenge of our time. According to the congressional Budget Office (CBO), in that year—the most recent year for which complete data are available—the 20 percent of households with the lowest incomes had an average pre-tax income of $25,000 while the 1 percent of households with the highest incomes had an

average income of $1.6 million. Roughly 15 percent of Americans lived in poverty . . ." (p. 151)

On the next page, the report states:

From his first days in office, President Obama has taken important steps to reduce inequality and make the economy work for all Americans. The policy response to the Great Recession directly reduced inequality in after-tax incomes through progressive tax and spending policies, such as temporary tax cuts for working and middle-class families. (p. 152)

President Obama was concerned about the big rise in income inequality and wealth concentration that had occurred during his administration and in previous years, and he tried to reduce this inequality through tax cuts for middle-class families. For the first time, a Keynesian style tax cut had occurred through a temporary fall in the social security tax. But his temporary tax cut made little difference to the huge rise in inequality caused by a jump in consumer and federal debt that occurred through the adoption of Keynesian expansionary policies. As Prof. Batra told me: "This is the biggest problem with neo-Keynesian policies. On the one hand, they create enormous debt at the consumer, state and federal level, and on the other they enrich the rich, and its proponents don't even realize that their own economic advice hands over vast economic and hence political power to the wealthy. Keynesianism gives pittance to the working families but offers a golden goose to the opulent."

Neo-Keynesian economists, such as Professors Stiglitz, Krugman, Sachs, and many others, are very critical of the wealthy one percenters for amassing vast amounts of wealth at the expense of the poor and the middle class, but they do not understand that their own advice is mainly responsible for the rise of one percenters. In this connection, two economists, Roar Bjonnes and Caroline Hargreaves, write:

Governments have been printing and borrowing money to stave off a collapse of the economy, but Batra claims that the only people to benefit from the huge budget deficits are the rich.

If there is a wage gap, then more goods are produced than can be bought. In this case, profits may actually fall. According to economist Ravi Batra, If consumer [or government] borrowing absorbs the unsold goods, business revenue rises by the amount of that borrowing and with wage cost staying constant or falling, the entire debt goes into raising profits by the same amount, provided the nation is not in a serious recession. The point is that monopoly capitalists always benefit hugely from so-called monetary and fiscal policies. (pp. 62–63)

Few economists blame American debt for extreme American inequality. Professor Stiglitz, for example, blames it mostly on rent seeking. In an article on this subject, he writes:

Thus, rent seeking means getting an income not as a reward for creating wealth but by grabbing a larger share of the wealth that would have been produced anyway. Indeed, rent seekers typically destroy wealth, as a by-product of their taking away from others. A monopolist who overcharges for her or his product takes money from those whom she or he is overcharging and at the same time destroys value. To get her or his monopoly price, she or he has to restrict production. (evonomics)

Professor Krugman blames inequality on other factors. He writes:

Disposable income in the United States is more unequally distributed than in most other advanced countries. But why?"

. . . The standard story up until now has been that the source of US inequality exceptionalism lies in the unusually low amount of redistribution we do through our tax and transfer system.

. . . We know that the US has unusually weak unions, low minimum wage, an exceptionally wide skills premium and, of course, an exceptionally imperial one percent. Shouldn't all this leave some mark on market income? (NYT)

The explanations offered by Stiglitz and Krugman are indeed valid, but according to the wage gap theory, they only explain that the wage gap has been rising. They do not explain why both income and wealth disparities have increased enormously even in a stagnant economy since 2007. Inequality cannot rise without a rise in debt. Even during the roaring 1920s, when Keynesian policies were unknown, inequality went up sharply because of the rising wage gap along with a rise in consumer debt. Unless goods produced by the rent seekers of Professor Stiglitz are sold, the producer cannot realize the fruit of the rising wage gap resulting from rising productivity and stagnant wages. And that requires a rise in debt.

6.6   Wage Gap and the Stock Market

Many economists have noticed that traditional macroeconomics does not offer a valid theory of the behavior of the stock market. Professors Stanley Fischer and Robert Merton conclude that "macro analysis should give more attention to the stock market." Stanford Professor Robert Hall, the president of American Economic Association in 2010, once said that "economists are as perplexed as anyone by the behavior of the stock market."

According to the wage-gap theory, a rise in the wage gap along with a rise in debt sharply increases the rate of profit. For example, in the numerical example in Section 6.4, when labor productivity rises from $8 to $9, the profit level rises from $200 to $300, provided the debt rises sufficiently so that there are no unsold goods. The rise from 8 to 9 is about 12 percent and a rise from 200 to 300 is 50 percent. In other words, a 12 percent rise in productivity generates a 50 percent rise in profits. Since the share prices are proportional to the level of profits, the stock market rises much faster than a rise in productivity. This is what happened during the dot-dot.com boom in the 1990s and perplexed economists such as Robert Hall. This is also what has happened since 2009 when the NBER declared the end of the Great Recession. People constantly wonder how the stock market breaks records in a stagnant economy. The answer is given by the constantly rising wage gap and the debt.

This is also what happened during the 1920s, when the wage gap rose sharply along with consumer debt (see Figures 6.5 and 6.6).

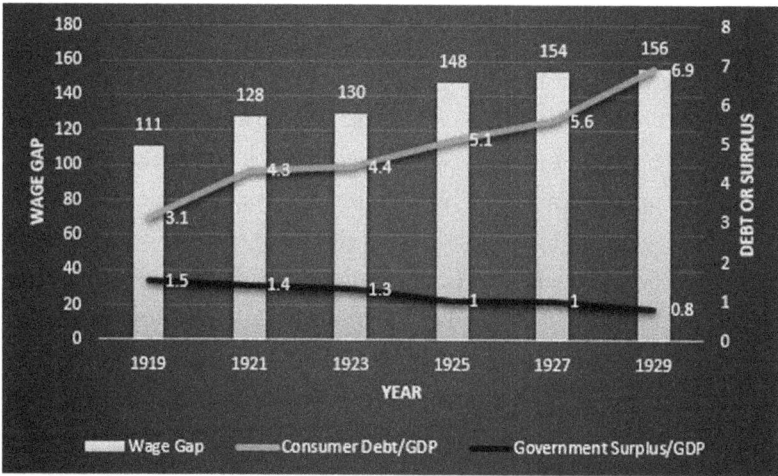

Figure 6.5 Wage gap, consumer debt, and budget surplus (in %): 1919–1929

Source: Batra, Ravi. *End Unemployment Now*, p. 69. Other Source: *Historical Statistics of the United States*, Series D68, D727 and D802.

Figure 6.6 Wage gap and share prices: 1919–1929

Source: Batra, Ravi. *End Unemployment Now*, p. 70. Other Source: *Historical Statistics of the United States*, Series X495.

6.7   The Stock-Market Crash

When the wage gap and debt go up for several years, the continuous rise in profits creates a stock-market bubble. A bubble may be defined as the case where people buy more stock even if stock prices rise. Normally, when the price of something rises, people buy less of it. But when people start buying more of some shares even with rising share prices, this means that they begin to take increasing amounts of risk. This creates inflated stock prices and a stock-market bubble is born. But every bubble has crashed in the past. The crashes of 1929, 1987, 2001, and 2008 had one thing in common. They all resulted from the bursting of a stock-market bubble.

The wage-gap theory says that every bubble crashes in the end. The reason comes from Batra's fundamental equilibrium equation that

Supply = Demand + Consumer borrowing + Government borrowing.

As long as this condition holds, producers are able to sell their output even if productivity rises faster than the real wage. This results in a sharp increase in profits, and when this happens over a long time, a bubble is born and no one expects the bubble to burst. Now the government borrowing can go on indefinitely. But consumer borrowing has a limit because the banks require reasonably good collateral to support their loans. Banks may be prone to taking greater risk in good times, but this cannot go on indefinitely. During the housing boom from 2001 to 2006, banks took big risks in home loans, but they still had some collateral underlying the loans. The collateral came from the value of the house even though some of these houses had inflated prices.

At some point in time, borrowers have used up their good collateral. At this point, banks cut their lending. As consumer borrowing falls,

Supply > Demand + Consumer borrowing + Government borrowing.

In other words, the value of production exceeds total spending and overproduction occurs. This causes a recession, layoffs, and a stock-market crash. Thus, bank lending creates a stock-market bubble and then bank restriction of lending causes a crash. This is how the stock market crashed in 1929 and later in 2008.

Sometimes, politics causes the government to cut its deficit or reduce the money supply. Here again supply exceeds spending to cause a recession and layoffs and eventually a stock-market crash. This is how a crash occurred in 2000 to 2001. Thus, according to the wage-gap theory, a stock-market bubble always bursts in the end.

6.8   Wage Gap and the Trade Surplus

The wage-gap theory also explains why a nation may adopt policies that create a constant trade surplus. This has happened in the case of many Asian countries such as China, Japan, and South Korea. It has also happened in the case of Germany.

As the wage gap rises, supply exceeds demand. Unless the government and consumers borrow enough money to raise spending to the level of supply, there is over production and layoffs. But suppose a nation's consumers are unwilling to borrow money and go into debt. The rates of savings are very high in China, Japan, and South Korea. Their people do not want to get into the debt habit. These nations then seek to send their excess production abroad, which becomes their trade surplus. In order to maintain a constant trade surplus, they constantly devalue their currencies relative to the dollar. The devaluation may be done openly or through purchase of American assets, especially U.S. government bonds.

With the help of dollars acquired through their trade surplus, the governments of trade surplus nations create artificial demand for the dollar so that the dollar remains an overvalued currency. Thus, the wage-gap theory explains why nations like China and Japan have constant trade surpluses while the United States has constant trade deficits.

6.9   Reasons for the Rising Wage Gap

There are many reasons for the rising wage gap and most of them are well known. Professor Stiglitz has noted some of them and Professor Krugman has written about others. Anything that lowers demand for workers and raises labor supply tends to reduce the real wage and raise productivity. The following are some important reasons for the rising wage gap in the United States:

1. Mergers after mergers have occurred in almost all industries. As a result, most industries have become oligopolies with large monopoly power for their dominant firms. The most famous merger is the one between two large oil firms such as Exxon and Mobil that became Exxon-Mobil in 1998. In 1911, they have been formed from the break-up of one company named Esso Oil. But the anti-trust laws are no longer enforced so mergers among large and profitable firms have become common since 1980. Each time a company merges with another, not only competition falls in that industry but also a large number of employees are fired. The result is a rise in productivity and a fall in the real wage. So, the wage gap goes up.

2. Another reason is a huge fall in the real minimum wage since 1969. About 20 million workers earn either a minimum wage or have their wages tied to it. The falling minimum wage, along with a rise in productivity, is a big reason for the rise in the wage gap.

3. Rising foreign competition is another reason that has lowered the influence and membership of labor unions. With a decline in union power and a rise in monopoly power of companies the wage rate no longer keeps up with rising prices. So, the real wage falls for production and non-supervisory workers, who are more than 75 percent of the labor force.

4. The constant trade deficit since 1980 has sharply lowered the importance of manufacturing in the U.S. economy, and manufacturing used to pay higher wages than other sectors such as the government and services.

5. Finally, some economists argue that rising productivity resulting from new technology offered by computers, robotics, and so on, lowers the demand for labor relative to labor supply. Thus, productivity rises but the real wage may fall. Such is the argument made by Abel and Bernanke. Many others have made a similar argument. The ultimate result is a rise in the wage gap.

6.10   Policy Implications

The wage-gap theory does not believe in neo-Keynesian economic policies that call for a rise in government and consumer debt whenever unemployment tends to rise. Such policies are desirable only in an economic emergency like that of the Great Depression or the Great Recession. Keynes never wanted a constant budget deficit. He said that the budget deficit was needed in a serious recession or depression, but once the economy recovered there should be a budget surplus. Thus, there is no need for a balanced budget every year, but the budget should be balanced over the course of the business cycle. Thus, neo-Keynesians have not been good followers of their leader.

The wage-gap theory believes in the policies of Adam Smith. The state should create competition in all industries because competition keeps prices low and wages high. The state should also take care of a nation's defense and infrastructure. In addition to Smith's policies, the wage-gap theory also believes that the minimum wage should be large enough so that a worker can afford at least the basic necessities of life such as food, clothing, shelter, education, and health care. This will keep government spending low on welfare.

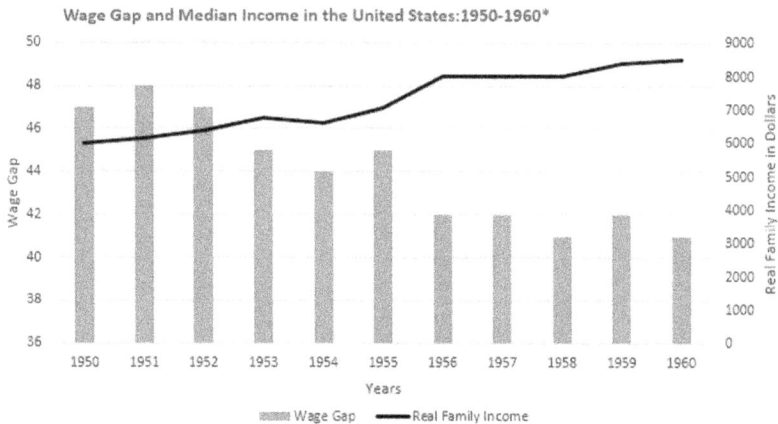

Figure 6.7 *Wage gap and real family income in the 1950s*

Source: Batra, Ravi. *End Unemployment Now*, p. 139. Other Source: *Historical Statistics of the United States, Series X495* (* Median Income is also known as real family income).

Unlike Keynesian economics that calls for stabilizing aggregate demand through automatic stabilizers, the wage-gap theory believes in stabilizing the wage gap. The two decades in which this gap was low and stable were the 1950s and the 1960s. In both cases, the U.S. economy grew strongly, and the middle class prospered. During 1950s and 1960s, a family could easily afford the necessities of life such as food, shelter, clothing, education, and health care without going into much debt. Consumer debt was low, and so was the federal debt.

Figures 6.7 and 6.8 illustrate these points graphically. Figure 6.7 shows that during the 1950s, for instance, the wage gap actually fell slightly and the real median income rose sharply and reduced poverty. However, the rate of profit was also low, as shown in Figure 6.8, but still it was adequate to keep the economy close to full employment. The 1950s ended up in a short recession, but the real median income kept rising. So, there is strong evidence of at least two decades that when the wage gap is stable, the middle-class benefits from rising productivity, and the government did not have to resort to debt creation to maintain prosperity.

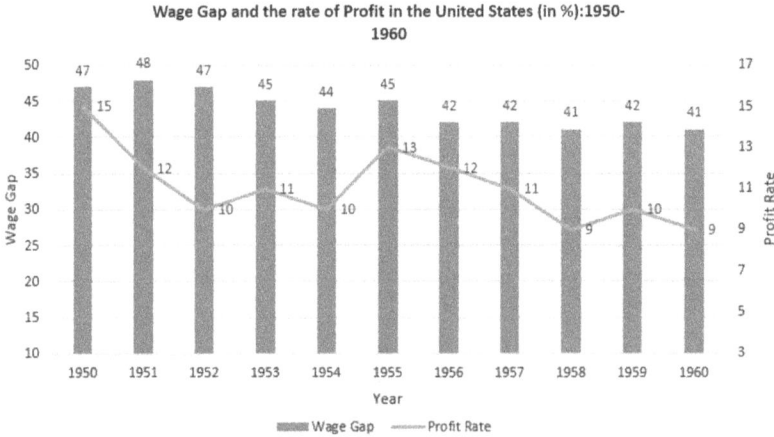

Wage Gap and the rate of Profit in the United States (in %):1950-1960

Figure 6.8 Rate of profit in the 1950s

Source: Batra, Ravi. *End Unemployment Now*, p. 141. Other Source: Council of Economic Advisers, *The Economic Report of the President*, 1975.

Bibliography

Abel., Andrew B., Bernanke, Ben. *Macroeconomics*. Addison Wesley, New York, 1995, p.89.

Batra, Ravi. *The Crash of the Millennium: Surviving the Coming Inflationary Depression*. 1st edition, Harmony, New York, 1999.

Batra, Ravi. *Common Sense Macroeconomics*. Liberty Press, Richardson, 2003.

Batra, Ravi. *The New Golden Age: The Coming Revolution against Political Corruption and Economic Chaos*. Macmillan, New York, 2009.

Batra, Ravi. *End Unemployment Now: How to Eliminate Joblessness, Debt and Poverty Despite Congress*. Palgrave Macmillan, New York, 2015.

Bjonnes, Roar, Hargreaves, Caroline. *Growing a New Economy: Beyond Crisis Capitalism and Environmental Destruction*. InnerWorld Publications, Puerto Rico, 2017.

Doshi, Navin. *Economics and Nature: Essays in Balance, Complementarity and Harmony*. Nalanda International, Los Angeles, 2012.

Krugman, Paul. *The Conscience of a Liberal. Explaining US Inequality Exceptionalism*. The New York Times. May 4, 2015. https://krugman.blogs.nytimes.com/2015/05/04/explaining-us-inequality-exceptionalism/

Merton, Robert C., Fischer Stanley C. *Macroeconomics and Finance: The Role of the Stock Market*. The National Bureau of Economic Research. March 1984. http://www.nber.org/papers/w1291

Mulay, Apek. *Mass Capitalism: A Blueprint for Economic Revival*. Book Publishers Network, Bothell, 2014.

Norris, Floyd. *Corporate Profits Grow and Wages Slide*. The New York Times. https://www.nytimes.com/2014/04/05/business/economy/corporate-profits-grow-ever-larger-as-slice-of-economy-as-wages-slide.html

Robert Hall, "Struggling to Understand the Stock Market," *American Economic Review*, May 2011, pp. 1–11.

Stiglitz, Joseph. *Econ Nobelist Joseph Stiglitz Says Standard Economics Is Wrong. Inequality and Unearned Income Kills the Economy*. Evonomics: The Next Evolution of Economics, July 29, 2017. https://www.facebook.com/notes/evonomics-the-next-evolution-of-economics/econ-nobelist-joseph-stiglitz-says-standard-economics-is-wrong-inequality-and-un/1930820927188687/

Thorgeirsson, Thorsteinn. Wage Productivity Gap and Economic Stability. *Visbending*. 2017; 35.

CHAPTER 7

The Wage Gap and the Future of the Technological Sector

7.1   Introduction

Most experts in economics nowadays fear new technology. The rapid automation that is happening in the industrial sector is a cause of concern for many policy planners because of the unemployment that results when automation displaces workers. As a technologist, I certainly want technology to advance continuously, and I believe the role of technological progress should be to ease the lives of human beings through automation of strenuous and repetitive operations. A productive use of technology happens when machines ease the lives of human beings with automation. However, as a macroeconomist, I am equally concerned about ensuring full-employment opportunities for the sake of economy. Hence, I must balance my dual professions when putting forth macroeconomic policies that would help in ushering the progress of technology as well as the growth of the economy. We must plan our economy such that technology can continue its progress forever, while this progress enhances the consumer purchasing power in the economy so that human beings want further technological progress.

This chapter throws further light on the wage-gap theory and highlights its impact on the broader technological sector. It highlights the problems resulting from the growth in the wage-productivity gap for the entire technological sector and the broader economy, which essentially supports the thesis that for exponential productivity gains that can be achieved with new technological developments, the wages in an economy should catch up with productivity gains that are achieved from the use of machines. A failure to do so results in a tremendous loss of productivity because of a slowdown in the overall technological sector. This chapter also sheds light on economic problems that would result from the introduction of universal basic income (UBI) as proposed by several well-known personalities in the tech sector, for example, SPACEX founder Elon Musk and Facebook founder Mark Zuckerberg. The advancement in technologies has shaken not only the tech sector CEOs but even the Federal Reserve Chair, Janet Yellen, who recently acknowledged that advancements in technology and globalization are chipping away at America's middle class. In this regard, it becomes mandatory that we find a solution to this crisis so that humanity can continue to benefit from technological progress.

7.2   Wage-Gap Theory Explains the Premature Demise of Moore's Law and Collapse of G450C

In the trilogy that I authored in three consecutive years 2014, 2015, and 2016, I have analyzed the past, present, and future of the semiconductor industry and Moore's law in the context of U.S. macroeconomic policies. In the 2014 work entitled *Mass Capitalism: A Blueprint for Economic Revival*, I analyzed the U.S. macroeconomic policies since World War II and concluded why the free-market theory of *mass capitalism* would ensure a swift revival of the U.S. semiconductor industry and the broader U.S. economy. I analyzed the problems in the broader U.S. economy and their impact on the progress of the semiconductor industry as a result of a growing gap between wages and productivity since 1971, as demonstrated clearly in Figure 7.1.

In 2015, my volume *Sustaining Moore's Law: Uncertainty Leading to a Certainty of IoT Revolution* explained the importance of a three-tier business model to sustain the progress of Moore's law and to usher the IoT revolution by learning from the mistakes made in the past. It also addressed the concerns of several CEOs in the semiconductor business and provided practical solutions to sustain progress in the semiconductor industry and overall technological sector.

Index, 1947=100 (log scale)

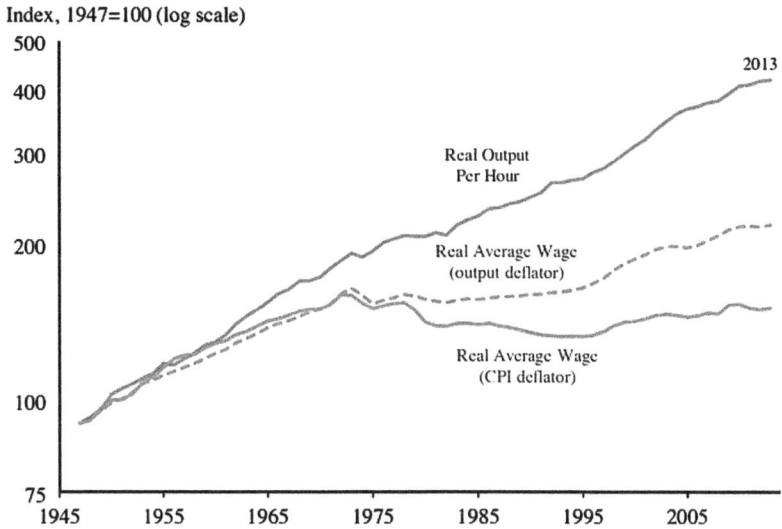

Figure 7.1 *Growth in productivity and average wage (1947–2013)*

Source: Council of Economic Advisers, *The Economic Report of the President*, 2014.

In my 2016 book, *How the Information Revolution Remade Busi-ness and the Economy: A Roadmap for Progress of the Semiconductor Industry*, I put forth a complete eco system to prevent loss of jobs due to ever-growing automation in the technological sector. In this book, I clearly demonstrated the tremendous deflationary impacts that 50 years of progress of Moore's law has had on U.S. economy and justified the importance of sustaining these deflationary impacts far into the future within the context of the wage-gap theory as elaborated in my previous two volumes. I also put forth the concepts of *Minimum Necessities* and *Maximum Amenities* as new drivers for achieving a better macroeconomic growth and to sustain the progress of *More-than-Moore and Beyond Moore* drivers put forth by International Technology Roadmap for Semiconduc-tors (ITRS).

My last three books have clearly demonstrated that in order to achieve a sustainable progress of the technological sector, it is critical that real economic demand should grow in proportion to growing supply of goods. As growth in supply comes from the productivity of the workforce and the growth in demand comes from the growth in wages, as long as wages keep pace with productivity, there is adequate demand to meet the growing supply of goods in the economy. However, as productivity grows exponentially due to rapid progress of Moore's law, the exponential growth in supply needs exponential growth in demand or new macroeconomic policies are needed, so as to maintain an economic balance. As wages have been stagnating as depicted in Figure 7.1, the Moore's law is coming to an early demise in U.S. and global economy. Figure 7.2 shows the complete semiconductor ecosystem for envisioning a sustainable Industry 4.0 having a true free market economy.

7.3   Industry 5.0 with Artificial Intelligence

Although artificial intelligence (AI) is Industry 5.0, which is said to be the future of new technology, it is already happening as I write this chapter. While the topic of AI and its impacts on the economy shall be covered in depth in Part II of this volume, in order for AI to avoid creation of unemployment in the economy, there have to be economic reforms toward a balanced economy that help reduce working hours during economic downturns and increase them during economic boom to restore economic equilibrium. Additionally, there has to be a transition to an economy which focuses on increasing human happiness by means of having

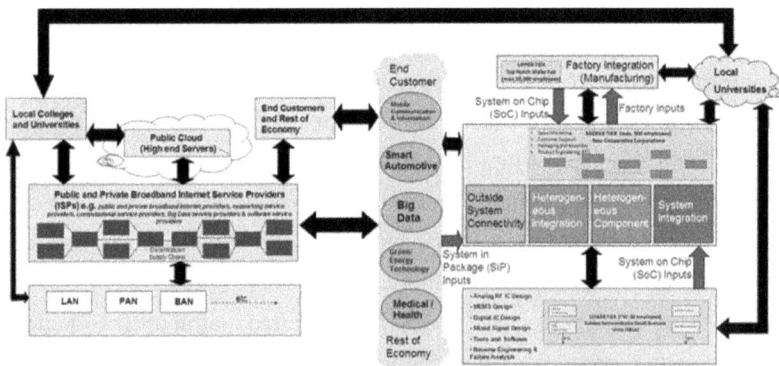

Figure 7.2 The semiconductor ecosystem for envisioning Industry 4.0

Source: Mulay, Apek. How the Information Revolution Remade Business and the Economy.

an understanding of human psychology. Measure of economic growth should not just be based on growth in productivity but also measure on growth in mental and spiritual well-being of all individuals in society. These topics shall be covered in depth in the second part of this book.

7.4   Technology and Automation: Only Humans Need Apply

A productive use of technology happens when machines are used to ease the lives of human beings by means of automation. The role of technological progress should be to ease the lives of human beings through automation of strenuous and repetitive work. However, as a macroeconomist, I am equally concerned about ensuring full employment in the economy.

Every technology expert who wants to envision the future of Moore's law must have a broader understanding of both technology and macroeconomics. It is the poor macroeconomic policy that is resulting into a premature demise of Moore's law due to poor return on investment (RoI). Hence, for sustaining the progress of Moore's law and for envisioning the progress of the tech sector, we have to prepare our economy for a rapid growth in productivity of machines resulting from the rapid progress of Moore's law.

Anyone from the technology sector or semiconductor industry, who wants to understand what the future holds for our economy, would be well served by reading the thoughts of well-known macroeconomists that I have quoted in previous chapters.

For technological progress to continue in a sustainable way, only human beings should apply to jobs and benefit from the growth of technology in the new economy. When rapid automation leads to a rapid growth in productivity, this productivity can bring about a sufficient purchasing power for all human beings on this planet. Freed-up time could be used for leisure, research and development of future technological progress, training and preparation of the future workforce, efforts to increase human creativity, activities to eliminate poverty, and so on. For all these ambitious goals to be achieved, it is essential that the economy has to adjust with the changes in time and space. Only a *mass capitalism* based free-market economy can adjust to these changes in time and space as explained in my trilogy.

7.5   How Industry 4.0 Will Be Different from Previous Industrial Revolutions?

In 1763, James Watt invented the first steam engine. The technological contributions that a British Scientist named Watt made were essential in starting Industry 1.0. His invention created a need for more efficient steam engines that were faster, safer, cleaner, and even more economically functional. This made the industrial revolution to grow tremendously, with a faster engine, transporting more goods in a shorter amount of time, and contributing to a new era of prosperity in America. There was tremendous growth in productivity, and this is how *James Watt* increased the economic growth of the United States by starting Industry 1.0.

The process of mechanization based on water and steam power started in Britain in mid-18th century, but it lagged in its colony, America, due to scarcity of labor because of which there was a lack of investments in expensive machinery to transform the agricultural economy. Mechanization began in its first phase in America from 1790s to 1830s with *Samuel Slater* pirating the design technology to start first industrial mill in 1790, which enabled an increased speed with which cotton could be spun into yarn. Boston Associates hired female factory workers for their low wages, which eventually led to first strike among textile workers protesting wage and factory conditions in 1824 and expanded to a larger scale in the 1830s. There was an improved transportation system available for raw materials to reach the factories and for manufactured goods to reach consumers.

At the beginning of the 20th century, cars were luxury items, which typically sold for nearly $20,000, and only the very rich could afford them. With the introduction of the assembly line, Henry Ford revolutionized the automobile industry, and the cost of cars dropped to a few thousand dollars with mass production resulting from assembly line.

In this way, Henry Ford played a very important role in Industry 2.0 by making automobiles cheaper and more affordable for consumers.

Similarly, mass production has been the key driver of growth in the U.S. semiconductor industry. Observations of the economics of the mass production of silicon came from Intel's Gordon Moore. The invention of the transistor in 1947 and integrated circuit in 1958 launched the information technology (IT) revolution. As a result, IT replaced the need to transport people and products with information. Today, digital signal processing has enabled voice and image information to be digitized into packets and transported around the world. This has enabled people to communicate practically anywhere without having to be physically adjacent to one another. Thus, Industry 3.0 started in United States with the microelectronics revolution based on rapid progress of Moore's law, also known as Digital Revolution. Just as what the steam engine has been for the Industry 1.0, which occurred over 250 years ago and assembly line has done for Industry 2.0 more than a century ago, so does the semiconductor industry become a similar gateway to a new U.S. economy with an exponential growth in productivity. It is estimated that the microelectronics revolution in the semiconductor industry has had two to four times the relative impact on the U.S. economy that the railroad had over a comparable time.

The rapid expansion in credit from unregulated activities of 200-state chartered banks, which came into existence after the closure of the national bank started by Hamilton in 1791, helped to exacerbate an economic collapse in 1929, which resulted in a 10-year-long depression in the United States. Of course, the macroeconomic reforms that were undertaken during the Great Depression resulted in free-market capitalism with worker wages keeping pace with worker productivity leading to the highest prosperity in United States during the decades of 1950s and 1960s, which is considered a golden era of free-market capitalism in the United States. However, stagnant wages and consumer demand since 1981 are now bringing Industry 3.0 to a standstill.

Tremendous technological progress in the last half century of Industry 3.0 has exponentially grown productivity as well as increased automation to reduce the cost of operation for businesses. Now, the transistor count has been increasing at astronomical scales worldwide, contributing to higher productivity. On the one hand, ever-growing productivity has reduced requirements for manual labor through automation. But, on other hand, huge unemployment created from reduction of workforce due to automation, has reduced the consumer purchasing power and is indirectly hurting the RoI. This brings any further progress of technological sector to a standstill. Thus, Industry 3.0 is coming to a standstill in spite of ever-increasing productivity from growth in the production of transistors to astronomical scales.

For Industry 4.0 of the Internet of Things (IoT) to become possible with a rapid progress of technology, both supply and demand have to grow. The supply comes from the productivity of workforce and demand comes from their wages. Hence, free-market economic reforms have to be pursued which ensure that wages automatically catch up with ever-growing productivity, with minimal government intervention. To avoid automation from destroying jobs in an economy, free markets should ensure that working hours of workforce be reduced during the waning phase of economy and increased during its waxing phase by undertaking holistic free-market economic reforms based on theory of *mass capitalism*, by letting employees become majority shareholders of Fortune 500 corporations, which would solve myriad economic problems within the United States and across the world.

Without pursuing the above proposed free-market economic reforms, Industry 4.0 will never happen. Additionally, the technological productivity has to be properly utilized to avoid creation of unemployment because of automation so as to pave the path for Industry 5.0.

7.6   A Call for Reform: The U.S. Economy and the Semiconductor Industry

For a healthy economy, in the past the desired equation was

$$\text{Supply} = \text{Demand}.$$

With the wages trailing productivity since 1981, elected officials in the United States have been following what is known as expansionary monetary policy, which tempts people into larger debts. This eliminates unemployment as spending rises to the level of supply, because now,

$$\text{Supply} = \text{Demand} + \text{New consumer debt.}$$

The wage-productivity gap has been rising so fast that the government also had to raise its own spending and debt constantly, so that total spending matched rising supply. In this case:

$$\text{Supply} = \text{Demand} + \text{New consumer debt} + \text{New government debt.}$$

The culture of growth through debt creation started in 1981 under President Ronald Reagan. Growth increased at first, but then began to fall. Now President Donald Trump is following the same policies, and the result is bound to be the same.

We already know that there was a major tax cut in 1981. Preparing for the rapid expansion of markets expected out of that tax cut, Intel Inc. licensed its 80286 micro-processor to other manufacturers, including AMD, Fujitsu, Siemens, and IBM. There was a big boom in 1983, into the middle of 1984—and then the semiconductor world suddenly collapsed in late 1984 and 1985. The resulting crisis caused Intel to lay off its workforce and shut down several factories due to the lack of economic demand and resulting excess supply.

This analysis shows that for the technology sector to progress, policy makers have to find a way to reduce the national debt but not at the expense of U.S. employment. They will most likely search for answers to the following questions:

- How is the technology sector supposed to progress so that Industry 4.0 becomes sustainable?
- How can Moore's law progress if there is huge unemployment, and under-employment resulting in a potential economic collapse?
- Is it possible to eventually envision an economy where *More-than-Moore* and *Beyond CMOS Moore* drivers proposed by ITRS get implemented for the progress of the global semiconductor industry?

- Can technological progress solve the problem of unemployment created by automation?

Now let us observe how the progress of Moore's law can help in solving the problem of low wages and persistent unemployment in a global economy. In fact, low real wages are precisely what is bringing the progress of Moore's law to a standstill due to poor RoI. As an example, if we consider the number of transistors manufactured by Intel Inc. for every generation of the progress of Moore's law to contribute to "supply" into the economy and the consumer demand for them as contributor to "demand" for these transistors, then any unemployment would represent a loss of demand. Hence, based on the wage-gap theory for the semiconductor industry, we have

$$\text{Transistors supply} = \text{Productivity x (Employment in}$$
$$\text{semiconductors)}$$
$$\text{Transistors demand} = \text{Fraction of (nation's income)}$$
$$\text{Semiconductor profits} = \text{Price x Output} - \text{Cost of production} -$$
$$\text{Unsold transistors}$$

The supply of transistors is well documented from the consistent progress of Moore's law, which raises productivity and hence the supply or output of transistors. The demand for transistors depends on the nation's income, which in turn depends on the wage gap, because as the wage gap rises, unemployment may rise, unless enough debt is created in the economy. Even if enough debt is created, the debt multiplier falls as seen in Section 3.5. So, the nation's income does not rise as fast as the supply of transistors. As a result, the real demand for transistors has been less than its supply for a long time. Hence profits in semiconductor industry have been going down because unused transistors or unsold electronics reduce these profits sharply and sometimes produce losses. Figure 7.3 shows an evidence of growing Wage-Gap in U.S. semiconductor industry. Figure 7.4 shows the rising U.S. National debt from 1971 to 2012 and Figure 7.5 shows the rising transistor count with the progress of Moore's law from 1971 to 2012.

Labor Productivity, Employment and Compensation Trends in Semiconductors and Electronic Components

Note: Productivity, employment and compensation are presented here as indexes that represent their values at each year relative to the base year (1997)

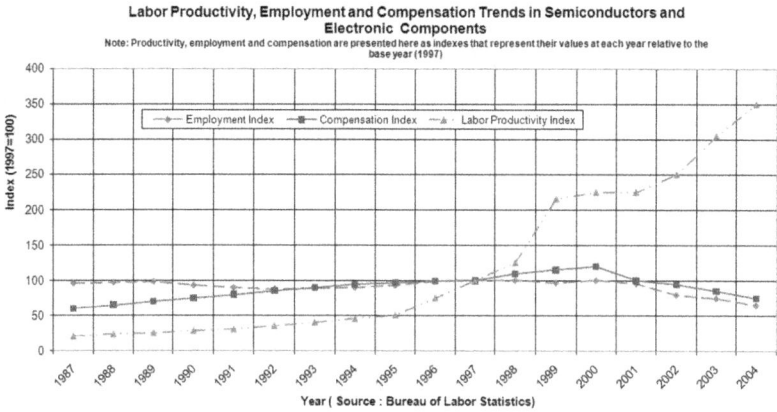

Figure 7.3 Wage gap in U.S. semiconductor industry (1997–2004)

Source: Mulay, Apek. *Mass Capitalism: A Blueprint for Economic Revival.*

U.S. National Debt (1971-2012)

Figure 7.4 Approx. U.S. national debt increase from 1971 to 2012

Source: Mulay, Apek. *How the Information Revolution Remade Business and the Economy.*

Every transistor that is manufactured contributes to an additional functionality on an integrated circuit (IC). This means that every ON/OFF action performed by a single functioning transistor contributes to a productivity increase. Hence, exponential growth in the number of transistors manufactured contributes to an exponential growth in functionalities on an IC which corresponds to an exponential growth in productivity in an economy. Thus, the supply into the economy had been growing exponentially, with the growth in the number of transistors making the electronic products much more powerful. The ratio of national debt per transistor measures the supply of transistors relative to debt-induced rise in spending. Since this ratio has dropped as shown in Figure 7.6, even the exponential rise in debt has not been sufficient to match the exponential rise in the supply of transistors in different manufactured consumer

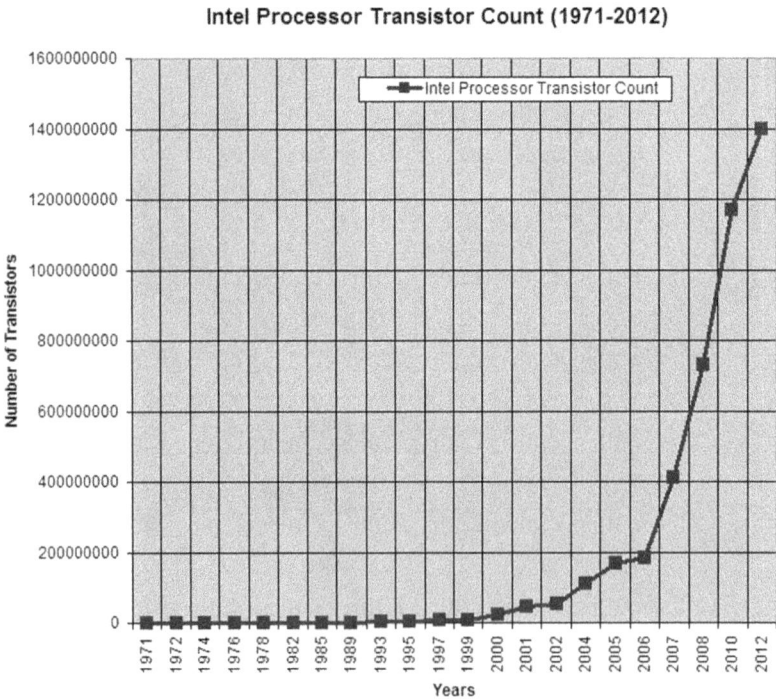

Intel Processor Transistor Count (1971-2012)

Figure 7.5 The increase in transistor count for Intel processors from 1971 to 2012

Source: Mulay, Apek. *How the Information Revolution Remade Business and the Economy.*

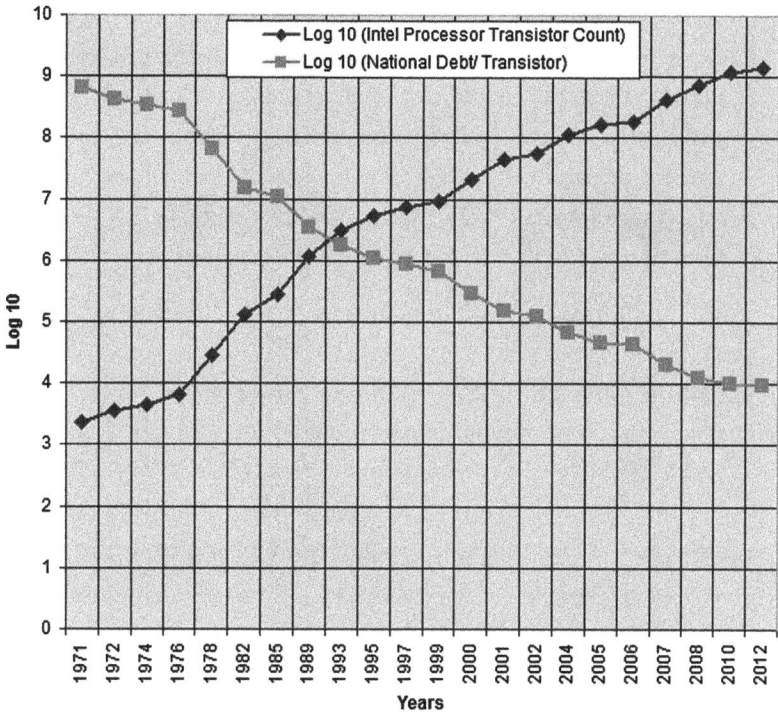

Figure 7.6 Deflationary impact of Moore's law on U.S. national debt

Source: Mulay, Apek. How the Information Revolution Remade Business and the Economy.

electronic products. This is further confirmation of why the semiconductor industry has lost its profitability.

As explained in Figure 7.6, we can observe that the ratio of national debt per transistor is steadily decreasing in the economy, which could be considered a deflationary impact of the progress of Moore's law on national debt. Because of reduced profitability, Moore's law is in trouble and the semiconductor industry believes that it could have an adverse impact on future productivity.

As it applies to the progress of Moore's law, the rising wage gap is responsible for the collapse of the 450 mm Silicon Wafer Consortium. At its inception, the Global 450 Consortium (G450C), a New York-based public/private program with a goal of building the 450-mm silicon wafers and equipment development environment, was a promising sign. In Chapter 8 entitled "The Macroeconomics of 450 mm Wafers" of my 2015 volume *Sustaining Moore's Law*, I stated:

This collaboration is first step forward by the global semiconductor industry to ensure a steady supply of 450mm diameter silicon wafers at a reduced cost. However, unless this consortium also ensures a similar collaboration and cooperation to generate a steady demand for this newly manufactured silicon, the huge capital investments made by the participants in the G450C consortium towards a transition to 450mm diameter silicon wafers cannot become sustainable. (p. 49)

Back in 2014, the initiative had strong leadership from its founding members: Global Foundries, IBM, Intel, Samsung, TSMC, and the College of Nanoscale Science and Engineering (CNSE). It is housed on State University of New York's (SUNY's) University at Albany campus and maintains a focus on "using wafers, equipment, people and cleanroom space to develop and test equipment to meet industry needs."

In that chapter, I mentioned about the urgency of having free-market economic reforms in order to allow semiconductor companies to justify their ever-increasing capital-intensive investments for transitioning to 450 mm diameter wafers. In 2015, I stated:

In order to sustain the progress of semiconductor industry which has been driven by the relentless progress of Moore's law, macroeconomic reforms have become critical to allow semiconductor companies to justify their ever-increasing capital-intensive investments for transitioning to 450mm diameter wafers. By establishing free markets, supply and demand of electronic goods would grow in proportion, thereby resulting in a balanced economic growth, low income taxes on individuals, higher investments, increased motivation for employees to work hard, and the growth of the overall economy. These free-market reforms seem to be the only path forward for global semiconductor industry to ensure its sustainability for transition to 450mm diameter silicon wafers.

When the G450C consortium collaborates to bring about such profound macroeconomic reforms, even if the future improvements in process technology for progress of Moore's law are less from one process generation to another, the macroeconomic growth in the overall economy would be very high. These reforms would ensure that the consumer purchasing power and hence prosperity of overall economy would be very high. With a high economic demand, the demand for the latest and greatest electronic products will continue to grow. In this way, the G450C consortium can ensure a good consumption of all manufactured silicon from larger size of 450mm diameter wafers. This robust consumer demand would force semiconductor industry to make more investments and manufacture latest and greatest electronic products to meet that growing demand.

In this way, mass capitalism based free-market reforms envision sustainability of huge capital investments in the transition to 450mm diameter silicon wafers. (Apek Mulay, *Sustaining Moore's Law,* p. 49)

At that time, I believed that global semiconductor industry did not take my advice seriously. In 2015, I made some additional bold forecasts and predictions about the uncertainty of the global semiconductor industry's ability to usher the IoT revolution in my book *Sustaining Moore's Law*.

Since 2015, we are in fact noticing more mergers and acquisitions (M&A) happening in the United States and global economy. I believe that these M&As violate antitrust laws and hence the global economy and U.S. economy (in particular) have continued to slowdown.

In 2015, we also saw a major crash of China's stock markets in the summer. Collaboration is critical for ensuring a robust growth in supply and demand for global semiconductor business and it is lacking in the current landscape. I was confident that the newly introduced drivers for the progress of semiconductor industry with *More-than-Moore and Beyond CMOS* would not achieve its desired goals of advancing Moore's law.

In a 2016 book published with Business Expert Press entitled *How the Information Revolution Remade Business and the Economy,* I offered a complete ecosystem for global semiconductor business to usher the Fourth Industrial Revolution while incorporating the new drivers for *More-than-Moore and Beyond CMOS*. A recently published article on

Extreme Tech entitled "450mm Silicon Wafers Aren't Happening Any Time Soon as Major Consortium Collapses," adds fuel to this conversation.

Because of the failure of the global semiconductor industry to take my macroeconomic analysis for 450 mm wafer silicon wafers, based on the wage-gap theory seriously, I believe that my ultimate forecast made in my 2015 volume is about to come true now and the collapse of the 450C consortium is an evidence of the same. As quoted from my 2015 book,

> Without above proposed macroeconomic reforms, progress of Moore's law seems impossible and chances of the U.S. economy transitioning from a great recession to a depression seems inevitable. (Apek Mulay, *Sustaining Moore's Law*, p. 49)

7.7   UBI Threatens the Future of Technological Sector

The CEO of Tesla and notable entrepreneur whom I had always admired as an engineer, Elon Musk, advocated that there should be UBI for people. He posited that it would lower the risk of backlash against the technology sector. A similar recommendation for UBI also comes from the Facebook Inc. founder and CEO, Mark Zuckerberg.

In spite of my admiration for Musk's tech skills, I believe that such a policy is going to be disastrous for the U.S. economy and even for the technology sector in the long term. In fact, I am surprised that a great entrepreneur and founder of companies like SpaceX and Tesla cannot envision the problems that his proposed policies are going to create for the U.S. economy and for the technology sector. The same thing also holds true for Zuckerberg, who mentioned about UBI at commencement speech at Harvard University.

First, the United States has a huge national debt of $20 trillion. Advocating dole-outs like the UBI will raise our national debt substantially. Just imagine if Tesla Inc. had to increase their corporate debt by a few hundred billion dollars every year. Without sufficient sales, the company would be unable to repay the debt on time. Who would be responsible for paying that extra debt? Musk's group of companies would. A failure to do so would affect his credit rating and reduce his credit line. In the worst case, the business might have to declare bankruptcy.

The United States is no different. A UBI would create huge debt and tax payers would have to foot the bill. Unfortunately, nobody wants to pay higher taxes in this economy. Perhaps tech company CEOs want to pay the additional tax personally (through, say, a UBI tax) for advocating UBI. I am sure that unemployed Americans would be delighted by their generosity in paying UBI taxes. I suspect, though, this answer would not be a popular one with technology leaders.

Instead, we have to realize that UBI is unsustainable for any economy. For a healthy economy, supply and demand are necessary. Supply comes from productivity of the workforce and demand comes the wages of the workforce. Hence, for a healthy economy, both the supply and demand must grow.

Automation and AI change this equation. If unemployment is created in domestic economy and the unemployed depend on doles like UBI and the number of the unemployed keeps growing, the creation of sustainable economic demand is compromised. Without sustainable economic demand, technology will not progress. Like any company, a company that caters to AI products needs more customers to increase its revenues. If AI increases the number of the unemployed, the UBI tax on taxpayers grows as well. This proposed UBI will likely create a backlash among the employed. Meanwhile, the unemployed will begin to depend on UBI for survival. Does Elon Musk and Mark Zuckerberg envision such an economy for America?

In a recent CNBC article published on July 27, 2017, entitled "Facebook Employees Living in a Garage Hope Mark Zuckerberg Will 'Learn What's Happening' in His Own City," a married couple working as contract workers in cafeteria of Facebook's Menlo Park, California, headquarters said in an interview with *The Guardian* that they can barely make ends meet. Together with their three children, Nicole and Victor share a two-car garage adjacent to Victor's parents' home. They borrow money from friends and family to stay afloat and occasionally resort to payday loans. Although they earn too much to qualify for state benefits, they don't earn enough to afford Facebook's health-care plan.

The above plight of Facebook's contract employees exposes the hypocrisy of Facebook Inc. founder Mark Zuckerberg. On the one hand, Zuckerberg does not ensure that employees and contractors who work at Facebook are paid sufficiently good wages so that all of them could live a good life and he expects the government to provide UBI to the unemployed. Well, if Facebook's compensation policies would ensure that they follow free-market economic policies such that wages keep pace with productivity of employees, neither would his employees have to live in garages nor would the government have to step into the role of spending money for UBI. This is because, in a free-market economy, the real job creators are both producers and consumers. The producers produce goods while the consumers consume these goods and hence a steady growth in consumer purchasing power in proportion to the growing productivity of workers keeps the economy in balance with a minimal government intervention.

I believe a free-market solution is better. Supply must balance with demand and only when both supply and demand grow will we sustain technological progress. A free-market solution enhances technological progress, increases quality of life for human beings, and leads to improved RoI. It would result in lower taxes and reduce the size of government too.

I would vehemently oppose any proposal to introduce UBI. As explained by Prof. Ravi Batra and quoted by several authors like Roar Bjonnes, any excess government spending goes into the pockets of the richest 0.1 percent Americans and just 5 percent of that spending reaches the people who really need help. In that case, a proposal to have a UBI would further enrich many at the top like Elon Musk and Mark Zuckerberg while further increasing poverty, unemployment, and the national debt of the United States.

A better free-market solution to this growing problem of unemployment created by automation has been provided in my volume *How the Information Revolution Remade Business and the Economy: A Roadmap for Progress of the Semiconductor Industry*. As there will be a lot of freed-up time because of automation, this time could be used for enhancing creative human pursuits.

The solution to all the world economic problems lies in the wage-gap theory of Prof. Ravi Batra. Hence, the technological sector can only progress by ensuring that wages grow in proportion to growing productivity. If technological sector productivity grows exponentially, then in order to restore the balance, the working hours of workers should go down during the waning phase of the economy and should increase during the waxing phase of the economy. In such an economy, there will be sufficient demand to meet the growing supply and hence there will be no problem of unemployment.

Bibliography

Hruska, Joel. *450mm Silicon Wafers Aren't Happening Any Time Soon as Major Consortium Collapses*. ExtremeTech. January 13, 2017. https://www.extremetech.com/computing/242699-450mm-silicon-wafers-arent-happening-time-soon-major-consortium-collapses

Kharpal, Arjun. *Tech CEOs Back Call for Basic Income as AI Job Losses Threaten Industry Backlash*. CNBC. February 21, 2017. https://www.cnbc.com/2017/02/21/technology-ceos-back-basic-income-as-ai-job-losses-threaten-industry-backlash.html

Martin, Emmie. *Facebook Employees Living in a Garage Hope Mark Zuckerberg Will 'Learn What's Happening' in His Own City*. CNBC, July 27, 2017. https://www.cnbc.com/2017/07/26/facebook-employees-living-in-a-garage-wish-for-zuckerbergs-help.html

Mulay, Apek. *Mass Capitalism: A Blueprint for Economic Revival*. Book Publishers Network, Bothell, 2014.

Mulay, Apek. *Sustaining Moore's Law: Uncertainty Leading to a Certainty of IoT Revolution*. Morgan & Claypool Publishers Network, San Rafael, 2015.

Mulay, Apek. *How the Information Revolution Remade the Business, and the Economy: A Roadmap for the Semiconductor Industry*. Business Expert Press, LLC., New York, 2016.

CHAPTER 8

Summation

If there was any doubt about the need for new macroeconomics, it has been removed convincingly by two articles published in September 2017. Ten years after the start of the Great Recession, Professor Stiglitz wrote a paper wondering "Where Modern Macroeconomics Went Wrong." He laid the blame on the use of extremely complex theories using extremely complex titles such as dynamic stochastic general equilibrium (DSGE) models that have found favor with economists today. These models have a lot of elegant math or econometrics, but very little in terms of new ideas. If Adam Smith were alive today, he would have a hard time understanding these models.

Two other economists, Eshe Nelso and Dan Kopf, commented on the Stiglitz paper and wrote an article entitled "Economic Models Are Broken, and Economists Have Wildly Different Ideas About How to Fix Them." They wrote:

> Ten years after the global financial crisis, economists are still puzzling over how they (mostly) failed to predict such a massive crash. Given all the data and experience at their disposal, how did they miss something so consequential?

It is true the economists today have a lot of information and high-powered tools of analysis, but they forget about the basic principles of supply and demand. Classical economics is in disrepute today, because almost every nation has intervened massively in its economy to contain the crisis, so much so that many nations even have negative interest rates. Before 2007, the idea of negative interest rates appeared laughable, but not anymore.

It is common for people to say that we are all Keynesians now, but economists forget that debt creation, which is what neo-Keynesian polices basically do, has its limitations, at least for consumers. Once families are burdened with debt, their borrowing is limited even at negative interest rates. Since consumer demand is the backbone of any economy, limited consumer demand means wage stagnation and low growth in spite of massive government deficits. This is what we have seen, and until we go back to some sort of *laissez-faire* where firms are more competitive, the world will not come out of its stagnation.

This is the message of my book.

The government intervention is desirable only in an emergency, but once the emergency is over, the government should enforce antimonopoly laws such as antitrust legislation and make sure that firms are no longer oligopolistic. This is the message of the wage-gap theory and I firmly believe in it. The wage gap is the difference between labor productivity and the real wage, and both should move together to have a healthy economy.

To summarize the contents in this book, we read in Chapter 1 some of the most popular theories before the Great Recession of 2007. Although, the neoclassical and Keynesian theories formed the bulk of material in that chapter, Chapter 1 also presented a brief account of various schools of thought of macroeconomics. By and large there are two schools—the interventionist and laissez-faire. Until about 1940, the laissez-faire school dominated economic policy, but after World War II, the interventionist school came to dominate it. However, since 2007, when the Great Recession started, the interventionist thought has become stronger even in academic circles.

In Chapter 2, we focused on where the global economy stands today in terms of economic growth, unemployment, debt, wage stagnation, inequality, and poverty. We observed the churning that has occurred in this field, understood the reasons behind this churning, and tried to understand why this churning continues to happen. We observed that the picture of the global economy does not look bright even though almost the entire world had printed vast amounts of currency and raised government budget deficits sharply since the start of the Great Recession.

In Chapter 3, we tried to understand the economic effects of income and wealth inequality. We began with the views of some well-known economists such as Professors Joseph Stiglitz, Paul Krugman, and Jeffrey Sachs, where we also tried to understand what these economists have in common and where they differ. This chapter also included the research of a few others such as Professor Ravi Batra. Our main conclusion here was that income and wealth disparities continue to rise even though economic growth has slowed down around the world.

In Chapter 4, we understood how the changing environment and macro policy interact with each other. It discussed a wide range of topics extensively such as gross national happiness (GNH), pollution taxes, subsidies, and so on, and the impacts of these topics on macroeconomic performance such as effects on jobs, economic growth, public well-being, and so on. It demonstrated the increasing awareness that economists have shown for an environmental-friendly macroeconomics since the start of the Great Recession. It concluded that although the phenomenon of global warming due to climate change still does not command full consensus, there is no doubt that global pollution continues to increase and so do its costs, especially in terms of mounting health problems all over the world. It hypothesized that people would choose a stable environment over continued growth and hence devised fiscal policies consistent with continued growth with pollution reduction.

Chapter 5 analyzed the reasons why central banks pay special attention to the effects of their policies on the stock market. While many economists concluded that they did not fully understand the functioning of stock market, this chapter analyzed some new theories that have emerged to answer their question. There are many theories of how stock markets behave over time; according to the efficient market theory, stocks are always priced at a fair market value and therefore a passive investment strategy is good for investors, and nothing is gained from frequent buying and selling of stocks. So is also the belief of the random walk theory. But there are those who believe in market timing and active management of their portfolios. Finally, the adaptive-market hypothesis believes that stock markets are rational and efficient most of the time, but when markets begin to fall, investors become emotional and cautious. They then adapt to the new environment

In Chapter 6, I focused on the wage-gap theory put forth by Professor Ravi Batra. I believe that this wage-gap theory answers all the questions that had been ignored by economists until 2007. This is a complete theory and it includes the best ideas from both classical and Keynesian models. Hence, this theory makes new macroeconomics really novel. As explained in this chapter, the wage-gap theory does not believe in constant application of Keynesian policies of printing money or keeping high budget deficits. However, it follows the advice of the father of modern economics, Adam Smith, and advocates the presence of high competition among firms to make them efficient and be responsive to the needs of the consumer. This chapter shows that Keynesian policies are not as effective as they used to be, and the wage-gap theory says that monopoly capitalism or a system of oligopolies is the culprit. Hence, we need free-market *Mass Capitalism.*

Finally, Chapter 7 discussed the implications of the wage-gap theory for the technological sector. It throws light on the tremendous slowdown in the technological sector resulting from the rising wage-productivity gap in the United States and global economy. It signifies the importance of the wage-gap theory for sustaining the progress of Moore's law, and for the success of G450C as well as to usher Industry 4.0.

In conclusion, the aftershocks of the Great Recession that started in 2007 are still there in some form, especially in the realm of poverty and destitution. A decade after the slump, poverty is higher than it was in the 1970s, while consumer debt in 2017 was the highest on record. A Bankrate.com study shows that more than half the people have less than $1,000 in savings. All these are the lingering effects of the recession. In the meanwhile, federal debt has risen by more than $10 trillion. This is what the neo-Keynesians have achieved. It is an enormous waste of capital and human resources.

We should all ask this question: Where have those $10 trillion gone? They have not gone to retirees, or workers, or the middle class. They have not uplifted the destitute. They have all gone into the pockets of multimillionaires and billionaires. Is this what the proponents of Keynesianism intended? If they did, then Keynesianism is useless to society; if they did not, then Keynesianism is a failed economic policy and should be discarded. It is time that we try the commonsense approach of the wage-gap theory of Professor Batra, whose forecasting accuracy since 2006 is almost 100 percent. He foresaw what no one else did. We should create competition in the economy. To paraphrase the late Nobel Laureate Milton Friedman, forecasting accuracy is the true test of any theory. The wage-gap theory handily passes this test.

In my first book, I talked about Mass Capitalism, which is the same system as Economic Democracy. That system should have universal appeal, because it includes the best features of various schools of economic thought. This is what I wrote then:

Economic democracy with economic decentralization should please the classical and neoclassical economists and the entire business community because of its small government. The neo-Keynesians would be happy because of low unemployment and inherent stability in the US economy. Because wages would catch up with productivity, there would be less inequality in the economy. In this way, there is not a single economic ill that cannot be solved by Mass Capitalism.

Bibliography

Mulay, Apek. *Mass Capitalism: A Blueprint for Economic Revival*. Book Publishers Network, Bothell, 2014.

Mulay, Apek. *Sustaining Moore's Law: Uncertainty Leading to a Certainty of IoT Revolution*. Morgan & Claypool Publishers Network, San Rafael, 2015.

Mulay, Apek. *How the Information Revolution Remade the Business, and the Economy: A Roadmap for the Semiconductor Industry*. Business Expert Press, LLC., New York, 2016.

Nelson, Eshe, Kopf, Dan. "Economic Models Are Broken and Economists Have Wildly Different Ideas About How to Fix Them," *Quartz*, September 14, 2017.

Stiglitz, Joseph. "Where Modern Macroeconomics Went Wrong," *Oxford Review of Economic Policy*, forthcoming. https://qz.com/1077549/economic-models -are-broken-and-economists-like-joseph-stiglitz-and-researchers-at-the -bank-of-england-have-wildly-different-ideas-about-how-to-fix-them/

About the Author

Apek Mulay is business and technology consultant at Mulay's Consultancy Services. He is also a senior analyst and macroeconomist in US Semiconductor Industry. He is the author of *Mass Capitalism: A Blueprint for Economic Revival.* He has other books such as *Sustaining Moore's Law: Uncertainty Leading to a Certainty of IoT Revolution* with Morgan & Claypool and *How Information Revolution Remade the Business and the Economy: A Roadmap for Progress of the Semiconductor Industry* and *New Macroeconomics* with Business Expert Press. His next book *New Macroeconomics in the Age of the Robot* is presently under authorship with Business Expert Press where he is collaborating with some experts across the world. He has also authored a monograph on technology with Lambert Academic Publishing entitled *Improving Reliability of Tungsten Plug Via on an Integrated Circuitry: Process Flow in BiCMOS and CMOS Technology with Failure Analysis, Design of Experiments, Statistical Analysis and Wafer Maps.* He is presently pursuing his second master's in business analytics with a specialization in marketing analytics at The University of Texas at Dallas.

Mulay pursued undergraduate studies in electronics engineering (EE) at the University of Mumbai in India and has completed master's degree in EE at the Texas Tech University, Lubbock. He authored a patent "Surface Imaging with Materials Identified by Colors" during his employment in Advanced CMOS technology development team at Texas Instruments Inc. He has chaired technical sessions at the International Symposium for Testing and Failure Analysis (ISTFA) for consecutive years. USCIS approved his US permanent residency under the category of foreign nationals with extraordinary abilities in science and technologies even though he did not pursue a PhD degree in engineering or economics.

Mulay has been cited as an "engineer-cum-economist" by superstar economist Professor Ravi Batra in his 2015 Volume End Unemployment

Now: How to Eliminate Poverty, Debt and Joblessness despite Congress. He is also a social entrepreneur and an investing partner in an e-commerce business http://calcuttahandicraft.in/ which he started to envision his ideas based on collaboration that he explains in his book Mass Capitalism. His blog is www.ApekMulay.com

Index

OTHER TITLES FROM THE ECONOMICS COLLECTION

Philip Romero, The University of Oregon and
Jeffrey Edwards, North Carolina A&T State University, *Editors*

- *How the Information Revolution Remade Business and the Economy: A Roadmap for Progress of the Semiconductor Industry* by Apek Mulay
- *Money and Banking: An Intermediate Market-Based Approach, Second Edition* by William D. Gerdes
- *Basic Cost Benefit Analysis for Assessing Local Public Projects, Second Edition* by Barry P. Keating and Maryann O. Keating
- *International Economics, Second Edition: Understanding the Forces of Globalization for Managers* by Paul Torelli
- *The Commonwealth of Independent States Economies: Perspectives and Challenges* by Marcus Goncalves and Erika Cornelius Smith
- *Econometrics for Daily Lives, Volume I* by Tam Bang Vu
- *Economics of Sustainable Development* by Runa Sarkar and Anup Sinha

Announcing the Business Expert Press Digital Library

Concise e-books business students need for classroom and research

This book can also be purchased in an e-book collection by your library as

- *a one-time purchase,*
- *that is owned forever,*
- *allows for simultaneous readers,*
- *has no restrictions on printing, and*
- *can be downloaded as PDFs from within the library community.*

Our digital library collections are a great solution to beat the rising cost of textbooks. E-books can be loaded into their course management systems or onto students' e-book readers.
The **Business Expert Press** digital libraries are very affordable, with no obligation to buy in future years. For more information, please visit **www.businessexpertpress.com/librarians**.
To set up a trial in the United States, please email **sales@businessexpertpress.com**.

www.ingramcontent.com/pod-product-compliance
Lightning Source LLC
Chambersburg PA
CBHW062006200326
41519CB00017B/4688